Buggy racing handbook

Buggy racing handbook

BILL BURKINSHAW

ARGUS BOOKS

Argus Books Ltd
1 Golden Square
London W1R 3AB
England

ISBN 0 85242 878 2

Phototypesetting by Photocomp Ltd., Birmingham

Printed and bound by A. Wheaton & Co. Ltd., Exeter

Contents

1   **Fast buggies**

Many people purchase radio controlled electric powered 1/10 scale buggies without any clear intention in mind. They have probably seen such models performing in a local park, or maybe they know someone that owns one, or have just been fascinated by the appearance of a kit in a local shop. Whatever route led to the purchase, once the model is together and running the 'bug' starts to bite.

The S.G. ¹⁄₁₀ scale buggy chassis, unusual in that it uses a longitudinally-mounted motor.

Trailing arm suspension is used on the four-wheel drive AYK *Viper.*

You're likely to be hooked very soon and looking for better perform- ance, other drivers to compete with and even more fun than you have already had just driving the buggy around your own back garden.

This book sets out to help the owner/driver who has succeeded in putting a buggy together, and getting it to run, to improve its perform- ance and his or her understanding of what makes the buggy work well. Successive chapters are devoted to detailed assembly techniques, motor performance checking and improving, speed controllers and R/C equip- ment, nicad battery checking and charging, setting up the buggy, com- mercial accessories and driving for racing success.

One thing that cannot be forgotten is that performance costs money. It is pointless to think otherwise. However well assembled and main-

The British Schumacher *Cat*, a robust belt-driven design introduced in 1986.

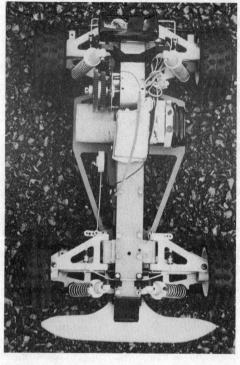

Automatic two-speed transmission is a feature of the P.B. *Mini-Mustang.*

tained your buggy is, if it is not fitted with ball-races, for example, it will always be that little bit slower than a similarly well prepared buggy that does have ball-races. Having said that, there are numerous areas that will benefit from simple care and without spending anything at all most buggies can be improved.

The first requisite for a fast buggy is proper assembly with all the various parts in top condition. It is a fair bet that if your buggy has seen much use, there will be a whole host of parts that need maintenance. For a start let's take the steering and see what areas demand attention.

Steering tune-up

Precise control of your buggy depends on the whole of the steering system accurately following the commands that you give using your R/C transmitter. If your buggy has seen quite a lot of use try the following test. Grip the front wheels individually and twist them as if they were

The prototype model for the P.B. *Mini-Mustang*.

steering and look carefully at the linkage between the wheel and the servo arm. You will almost certainly see the front suspension upright twist sideways a little, then the slop in the steering arm ball-joint will be taken up followed by the slop in the servo saver ball-joints. The servo saver may rock sideways on its pivot post, the slop in the linkage between servo and servo saver will now be taken up and the motion finally reaches the servo. Look very carefully here and you will probably see that the servo output arm moves fractionally before you are finally able to feel through the front wheels that all the free movement has

This 2WD Associated RC10 from the U.S.A. competes with the best of 4WD buggies.

9

Four-wheel drive chain transmission is used on the Kyosho *Progress* from Japan.

been taken up. How far could you move the steering before the resistance of the servo motor was felt?. Working from the opposite end, how far does the servo move before there is any effect on the steering of your buggy?

Convinced that the steering needs attention now?

Precision starts at the steering servo and the majority of owners start with a 'budget-priced' R/C system that will be supplied with what are usually called 'Standard' servos. Such servos may be splash-proof but are unlikely to be either fully waterproof, dustproof or ball-raced.

Additionally, the power output of the servo may be limited as the cost of adding the extra transistors to the servo amplifier to raise the power would raise the price of the servo. Centring of the budget servos can also be suspect. Centring ability is important, otherwise when you release the transmitter control sticks you will never be certain that the steering will go back to the same place. Also important is Resolution, the ability of the servo to follow the stick movements with precision. Cheaper servos will not be as precise in their ability in this area and may well move more in one direction than the other. You pay for top performance but the resulting equipment will last and perform better.

The lack of dustproofing can lead to very rapid wear of the servo output shaft resulting in unwanted free movement. A good quality ball-raced high speed, high power miniature servo is a very good investment here. It is certain that almost whatever R/C equipment you own, there will be a suitable replacement servo available. Further on in Chapter 6 there is a full description of how to fit and match servos of differing makes to most types of R/C equipment.

10

Although most R/C manufacturers do make a wide range of servo arms, few cater specifically for the buggy racers' needs. Frequently, to get sufficient steering movement, a very long servo arm has to be fitted and most so supplied with the servos will be too flexible. Heavy duty arms are made for the High Power servos made by R/C equipment makers for operating retractable undercarriages on model aircraft and these, or servo discs such as those made by PB Racing, should be substituted for the standard items.

Moving on from the servo to the servo saver and connections between the two, do make sure that the servo saver fits the servo output shaft properly, if it is of the type that fits directly onto the servo. If necessary, fit thin plastic sheet shims to the servo output shaft before fitting the saver. Another minor problem that is often overlooked here is that in some instances the servo saver can be tightened down onto the servo until the body of the saver rubs against the servo case, causing overloading and spoiling the resolution of the servo.

Next, take a look at the connecting rod between servo output arm and servo saver. This needs to be rigid, but there is a tendency in some four-

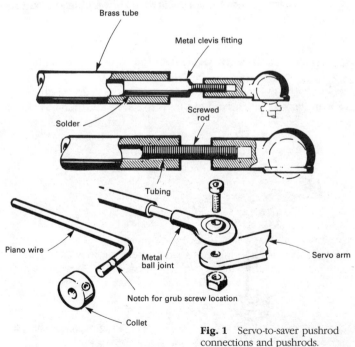

Fig. 1 Servo-to-saver pushrod connections and pushrods.

11

wheel drive buggies to position the steering servo fairly well back in the chassis, resulting in a long rod. Piano wire is a common material and 16swg is fine for pushrods up to 75mm long, but over that something a little more rigid is necessary. Tubular material is a good compromise, as heavier gauge wire starts to get heavy and difficult to bend. Aluminium tube is adequately strong but difficult to join. Several suggestions are shown in Figure 1. The actual connections to servo arm and saver need to be free-moving without slop, and if ball joints are used the ball can be polished to achieve a free movement. The Figure shows some possibilities.

Ball-races in the servo saver are a good idea and if the servo saver is fitted with metal or plastic removable bushes this is a very easy modification to make. Providing that there is enough material to support a ball-race the saver can be modified to suit. See Figure 2.

Track rods come next. Rigidity and free movement are once again essentials, good quality heavy duty ball-joints are needed and small aluminium alloy sheet retainers are well worth the trouble of fitting. See Figure 3. Once the whole linkage is overhauled the check that you made before starting should be repeated and a significant reduction in the free movement should be evident.

Suspension pivot points

Before making any attempt to modify suspension geometry, a series of checks similar to that carried out with the steering linkages should be

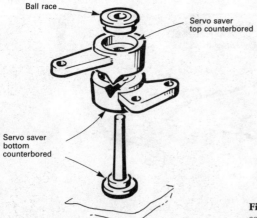

Ball race

Servo saver top counterbored

Servo saver bottom counterbored

Fig.2 Fitting a ball-race to the servo-saver.

Fig. 3 Retaining
bracelet fitted to a
ball-joint.

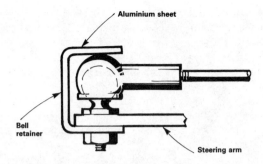

made on the pivots and joints. Both metal and plastic suspension arms suffer from wear and unless the fit is very good to start with wear can be very rapid. If there is a loose fit, grit soon gets into the spaces and grinds down the bearing areas.

Taking swinging arm style suspension first, many buggies that use this system have die-cast metal arms. If these are worn then they will either have to be replaced or fitted with plastic bushes. This is not such a difficult task; the holes through the arms should first be reamed or drilled oversize then a section of plastic material pressed in which can then be drilled or reamed to the correct size for the pivot pin. A useful source of plastic material is sold as Plastruct in many model shops, and this can be obtained in a range of diameters. Nor should the plastic sprue found in most kits be forgotten.

Although in metal a reamer is the ideal tool for finishing a hole to an accurate size, in plastic it is not as effective because the plastic tends to stretch while the reamer is passed through the hole and then relax to a

Suspension detail on
a P.B. buggy.

An example of four-wheel drive with shaft transmission is the Tamiya *Hot Shot.*

smaller diameter when the reamer is withdrawn. Using a drill 0,1mm or 0,2mm larger than the required size will usually result in a close fitting bush. See photos.

Once the arm is bushed and a good smooth fit, use shimming washers to adjust the end float of the arm. Ideally these should be from a PTFE or Nylon material but metal washers will do.

The most difficult areas to treat are ball joints, particularly those found on buggies such as the Tamiya 'Fox'. Sanding down the faces of the wishbone will allow the clamping plates to close up on the ball and remove slop. Once correctly set up avoid lubricating the joints but thoroughly clean them very regularly.

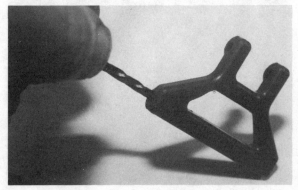

Drilling out a plastic wishbone to receive a bush.

14

Fig. 4 Metal bushing for wishbone joints.

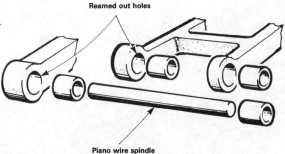

Reamed out holes

Piano wire spindle

Plastic wishbones that pivot on metal pins can also be bushed. There is a tremendous variety of brass tubing available from K & S Metal Centres which are found at many model shops and suitable sizes can usually be found. It may be necessary to replace the pivot pins with a size smaller so that a good fit of tube to wishbone can be achieved. In this case the mounting points in the chassis will have to be bushed as well as the wishbones. See Figure 4.

The easiest way to cut the brass tube is to roll it on the workbench under the blade of a sharp knife. Once it is scored, it will snap off cleanly and will only need a slight de-burring before the bush thus made is fitted.

Properly fitting suspension arms will just drop under their own weight without the wheels fitted and show no signs of sideways movement. It is important that pivot pins are straight: early Tamiya models such as the 'Super-Champ', 'Sand-Scorcher' etc., suffered from pivot spindles for the front suspension becoming bent and although these buggies have been superseded they are still available and often find

Cutting brass tube with a heavy-duty knife.

15

The Tamiya *Fox* features ball-jointed wishbones.

their way as second-hand bargains into beginners' hands. Several accessory manufacturers supplied hardened steel replacement pivot spindles and these are a worthwhile investment if they can be tracked down. On the same buggy, the U.S.A. manufacturer Thorpe produced a captive style pivot moulding for the swivels at the end of the suspension arms that prevents the ball joints from popping out.

Drive shaft end-float

While adjusting the free movement of the suspension arms using packing washers the opportunity should be taken of checking that the end float in the drive shafts is adequate. On all buggies which feature fully independent wishbone or trailing arm style suspension, the drive shaft has of necessity to be free to move in the drive sockets at least at one end. Carefully designed swinging arm suspension may use a drive shaft that is firmly anchored at each end, however. The drive shaft must have clearance or 'end-float' throughout the full range of the suspension movement and this end-float is normally at a minimum with the suspension at the centre of its travel. Around 0,5mm is enough and the suspension arms should be shimmed to provide this clearance. When checking do rotate the wheels through a full turn as if the drive shafts are fitted with ball and pin joints the pins may bottom in the slots and lock up the drive if the clearance is inadequate.

Such adjustments are more difficult with wishbone style suspension, but as there is less possibility of the drive shafts popping out in the first

Fig. 5 End-pads for drive shafts, cut from tyre spikes.

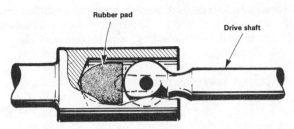

place, initial clearances set up by the manufacturer are usually more generous. However, take a close look at the way the drive shaft behaves as the wheels are turned with the suspension moved through its full range of travel. If the drive shaft looks as though it might possibly try to escape you may be able to fit a small pad or spring to keep it in a more central position. A slice from the top of the spike from a spiked tyre makes a very good pad! See Figure 5.

Drive shafts must be straight otherwise they will help generate vibration and contribute to rapid bearing wear even if ball-races are fitted. Roll the drive shaft on a flat piece of metal, the widest that you can find that will fit between the driving portions at the ends.

There are some very good moulded plastic drive shafts available which can, in common with many nylon moulded parts, benefit from stress relieving before fitting. Although some manufacturers now make a point of stress relieving parts before supplying, it does no harm to repeat the process. Simply drop the part into boiling water for a minute or two and the brittleness will be reduced dramatically. If you are unsure about any particular plastic's suitability for this treatment, try a piece of the moulding sprue from the kit before risking what could be an expensive part. Incidentally, if the parts are moulded in white nylon as in the Associated RC10 kits, then you can dye them at the same time by adding Dylon dye to the water to produce any one of a huge range of colours.

Wheel spindles and bearings

Plain bush bearings, be they bronze or plastic, wear very quickly when supporting wheel spindles. Even for front wheels ball-races are a must. Without them the precision of the steering will be hampered and, if your buggy is 4WD then drive efficiency will be doubly reduced. The plastic caged roller races supplied with latest model Kyosho buggies are a big improvement on plain bushes but the die-cast metal arms wear rapidly and ball-races need to be fitted early in the life of the buggy otherwise if the decision is left too long then they will not fit properly into the housings and not give maximum benefit.

Fitting ball-races

Most kit manufacturers are able to supply sets of ball-races to suit their products but if the kits are imported, and there are few that are 'home grown', then the ball-races are likely to be expensive. There may well be a ball bearing factor in your area and a look at the 'Yellow Pages' of your telephone directory could be beneficial. It is unlikely that the sizes required will be all that difficult to get but you may well find that there is a minimum order quantity and several people will have to club together to make up the order. Specify 'double shielded' races and measure carefully the outside diameter, through-hole size and thickness of the bearing. If there is a choice get stainless races (if you can afford them!) Figure 6 shows the vital dimensions of ball-races. If you are fitting ball-races it is only sensible to make sure that both the inner and outer parts of the bearing fit properly so that the ball-race works properly. It is quite acceptable for the bearing to be a very tight fit on the shaft that it is to support, but a loose fit is not a good idea, as there could be a tendency for the shaft to rotate inside the bearing. Likewise, the whole ball-race should be a firm press fit in its housing. Slightly loose fits can be improved by the use of a bearing locking compound or straightforward thread locking compound if the bearing is to go into a metal part. Beware of using thread locking compounds on plastic parts, as some plastics are adversely affected by the thread lock. If you have any doubts, use a fast-set epoxy glue to secure the bearing. Obviously, it is essential to take very great care not to gum up bearings with thread lock or epoxy when doing this!

If the bearing is a very tight fit on the shaft then it may be a good idea to polish the shaft with fine waterproof abrasive paper (wet-or-dry) of

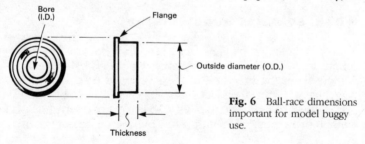

Fig. 6 Ball-race dimensions important for model buggy use.

First of the mid-mounted motor four-wheel drive buggies, the Yokomo *Dogfighter*.

about 400 grade using a little oil while spinning it in the chuck of an electric drill. Clean off all traces of the abrasive before assembling the buggy or it may find its way into the new ball-races.

For maximum benefit to be gained from the use of ball-races it is essential that they are fitted correctly, particularly with regard to alignment. Wherever possible use some form of pilot to guide the ball-race squarely into place – the actual spindle that it is to carry will usually

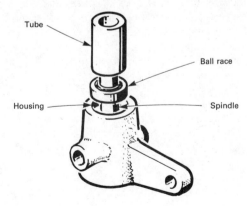

Tube

Ball race

Housing

Spindle

Fig. 7 Fitting a ball-race with the aid of a tube and mandrel.

do. See Figure 7. Avoid hitting ball-races but wherever possible squeeze them into place using a vice or clamp and suitable sections of rod and tube to apply pressure to the race where it will not do any harm. See Figure 7. A spindle that runs in a pair of properly installed ball-races should spin almost totally without friction: any sign of stiffness indicates that the races are not properly aligned.

Where the races are well protected from grit, inside gearboxes for example, a good quality lubricant can be applied. I have found the aerosol-dispensed motor cycle chain lubricants to be very good, as they are designed for very arduous duty and penetrate well into the races. For bearings in more exposed situations only apply the lubricant while in your workshop and then only after thoroughly cleaning the bearings to prevent dirt from being washed into the races. Follow up by removing every trace of oil from the bearing exterior before running your buggy. Any oil on the outside of the race will attract dust and grit and soon promote wear of the race.

Motors

2

Motors for buggy racing, or any other form of electric powered racing come to that, along with the nicads, are the most argued-about elements of the whole car. It seems a simple enough problem to resolve until one realises that the range of variables in both methods of construction of the motor and materials used in it have very wide-ranging effects on the performance of the buggy, while there seems to be an overwhelming feeling that the motors should be cheap to buy.

Quite why this particular attitude exists is difficult to understand when one considers that a significant percentage of buggy drivers are

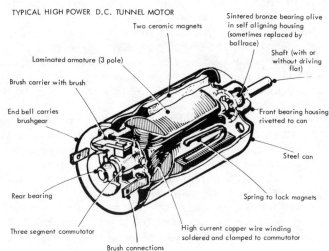

TYPICAL HIGH POWER D.C. TUNNEL MOTOR

Two ceramic magnets

Sintered bronze bearing olive in self aligning housing (sometimes replaced by ballrace)

Laminated armature (3 pole)

Shaft (with or without driving flat)

Brush carrier with brush

End bell carries brushgear

Front bearing housing rivetted to can

Steel can

Rear bearing

Spring to lock magnets

Fig. 8
Motor parts.

Three segment commutator

High current copper wire winding soldered and clamped to commutator

Brush connections

The Igorashi motor, which has a good reputation.

prepared to pay approaching £200 for their buggy, then look upon 10% of that as an excessive amount of money for a motor. There is a wealth of truth in the old saying that goes along the lines of 'you get what you pay for' and there is no doubt at all that for many years the incredibly cheap motors that were used for all forms of R/C car racing were wildly variable in performance. This forced those who wished to be competitive to purchase several motors to find a good one. Additionally these cheap motors were impossible to repair or even service as they were 'permanently' closed upon factory assembly.

Good quality motors always were available, but at a price and also sold under the label of 'Modified' motors. The actual performance of these modified motors was not always the attraction to the enthusiasts who pushed for their overall adoption for general racing. By far the most important reason for their pressure was that they had found by extensive use of such motors that they were more consistent in performance, more reliable, longer lasting and generally far better value for money. Most of the so-called modifications to the motors were little more than the same modifications that every driver performs on his buggy as a matter of course – fitting ball-races, polishing up the working parts, balancing and building in a provision for adjustment.

At the root of the arguments against the modified motor was a fear that by allowing the use of 'Modified' motors it would become possible for the unskilled competitor to 'buy success' in the form of super-powered motors, forcing an upward spiral of cost on the majority of drivers. There is no doubt at all in my mind that this particular argument is totally without logical foundation. There is so much more

A typical Mabuchi-produced motor for buggies.

to winning a buggy race than just fitting an expensive motor and in very many instances the driver who is disappointed with his lap times would probably be far better advised to drive a *slower* buggy more carefully and achieve fast times by consistent driving than attempt to crush the opposition with a powerful motor. The most likely result is that he will simply crush the track markers! In the long run it makes far better sense to limit motors by carefully considering specification rather than setting cost limits and by so doing believing that all drivers will have an equal chance. This is not and never will be so. Drivers should be graded by ability, not depth of pocket, with races run to provide sporting challenges for all levels of ability.

Consumer demands for better motors have at last enabled manufacturers to invest in the production of significantly better motors at modest prices, such as the Yokomo, Mabuchi Techniplus and Kyosho types, all with the features once found only in 'modifieds'. Of course these motors can also be modified to advantage and are found in varying specification levels from both original manufacturer and tune-up specialists. A typical general arrangement of the motor type finding wide acceptance for buggy racing is shown in Fig. 8, which also serves to indicate all the vital parts of the motor.

Choosing and using your motor

Like it or not, the style of racing organised in the UK currently separates into two classes based on motor specification and cost. Standard Class

23

Two Kyosho motors;
the left-hand one is
ball-raced.

racing uses a motor with a specification (at the time of writing) as
follows:
  (i)   Only nationally commercially available motors may be used;
  (ii) The maximum retail price of the motor will be £12;
  (iii) Only unopened, permanently factory-sealed motors may be
        used;
  (iv) Brushes and brush springs may be replaced by manufacturers'
        spare parts;
  (v)   Only one drive motor may be used.
    Although it is generally assumed, Rule (i) does not actually say that
there are only Mabuchi, Igorashi and Yokomo-made motors to be used
and anyone who was able to find a ball-raced, 'computer balanced'
super-duper motor for under £12 whatever the size, providing that it

One of the range of
more than a dozen
Yokomo motors.

Similar motors can be found under different labels, possibly with different brush gear etc.

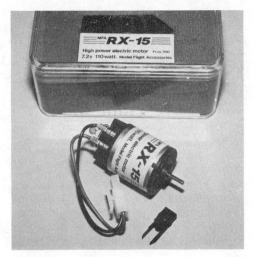

would fit into the buggy, could use it! Modified motors come under a similarly loosely-worded control. The limiting factor in this instance is the retail cost of £35 maximum, thus allowing the keen racer to purchase a £5 motor and spend £500 on making his own modifications.

For most racers, however, the choice will be simply between purchasing a Standard or Modified motor and for the Modified motor, just how far up the ladder to the full £35 limit they are prepared to go. Motors used do follow fashion to some extent and as time goes by im-

Dropping a running motor into cleaning fluid may seem drastic but it is highly effective.

25

provements are made, leading to genuine differences between this year's top motor and next year's. By and large whatever Standard motor you choose its performance will be broadly similar to all the others. How you prepare, maintain and treat it will be the keys to your success or otherwise.

Remember that if you have a Standard motor and wish to race at Open race meetings away from your local club, any evidence that the motor has been dismantled will lead to disqualification. Even if you were so clever as to succeed in taking the motor to pieces and putting it back together again without leaving any tell-tale signs, if you have managed to improve the performance significantly the Race Scrutineer may well decide to take your motor apart and look for signs of modification. The short answer is don't cheat! There is more satisfaction to be gained from winning fairly. By properly preparing your motor there is likely to be more benefit than by unskilled modification anyway.

Clean it up

Firstly the motor should be cleaned. That's right, cleaned. I use a proprietary cleaning fluid made by Bo-Link of the USA, but there are several suitable products on the market. I suggest that you use the fluid in a good-sized glass jar, the sort of thing that is found in kitchens for storage of dried fruit etc. The neck has obviously got to be large enough to drop the motor through whatever you choose. Firstly, fit your chosen connector to the motor and find a battery pack that is fairly well discharged, though it needs to have enough 'urge' to spin the motor steadily. Connect up and lower the spinning motor into the cleaning fluid for a few seconds, giving it a fairly thorough agitation at the same time. I would be surprised if the fluid remains clean after this process, as there will almost certainly be small metal particles and other dust and dirt swilled out of the motor. Allow the cleaning fluid to evaporate from the motor and seal the cleaning jar while the dirt settles to the bottom of the jar. Once it has settled you will be able to decant the clean fluid

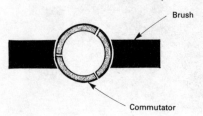

Brush

Commutator

Fig. 9 Brushes should be bedded to the commutator over their full area for maximum performance.

carefully back into the original container and throw away the dirty dregs ready for cleaning your motor again in the future.

Take advantage of the opportunity afforded by external brush gear (if your motor has it) to set the spring pressures and provide free movement for the brushes. Free the brush springs and test for free movement of the brushes. The most likely cause of stickiness is the corners of the brushes which may be very lightly scraped with a sharp scalpel until they slide freely in their carriers.

Ideally use a spring balance on the free end of the brush spring to set the pre-load. The most important factor is uniformity of pressure: you can experiment later to find the results of varying the pressure.

If you are using a motor with enclosed brush gear your motor should be run in. No matter what quality of product you are using it will benefit from a period of unstressed bedding-in for bearings and brush gear. Good contact between brush and commutator is vital if the motor is to perform well. See Fig. 9. There is a lot to be said for water-dipping motors as an aid to fast running in. Even if the manufacturer claims running in is not necessary, you may just have got the one motor from the batch of 500 that failed to go through that vital step of the manufacturing process. For the sake of five minutes' work you will know that the job has been done well. Take your clean motor and apply a small quantity of lubricating oil to the bearings, turning the motor by hand to work it into the bearings. Now find a suitable container for some clean water (you could use the same glass container that you used for the cleaning fluid) and using that same run-down battery pack, hook up the motor and while it is spinning over dip it into the container of water. Watch carefully and as soon as you see cloudy evidence of the brushes wearing

A trace of special electrical lubricant on the brushes is worth a few extra r.p.m.

27

down emerging from the motor, disconnect and remove the motor from the water. If you carry this process on for more than a few seconds the brushes will be ground away to nothing.

Dry off the motor externally and place in a warm dry place for sufficient time for all traces of moisture to evaporate. Now re-clean and apply oil to the main bearings followed by a commutator treatment such as 'Mr Cool' and your motor is ready for use. All you need to do now is treat it properly and it will give you good service for quite some time to come. Running-in of motors with external brush gear is not usually reckoned to be needed. As the brushes can be so easily changed a much softer grade of brush can be used which beds in very quickly.

A modified motor can be prepared in exactly the same way as the Standard motor preparation described above. If the motor has been modified by a specialist such as Reedy or MG then it will almost certainly have been treated to the above procedures and can be used straight from the box. However, if the motor is a High Spec mass-produced product from Kyosho, AYK etc. then it will benefit from the Standard treatment.

Maintaining good performance

So much for new motors. What about keeping them in good order and finding out if the one you have got is any good? The enemies of small permanent magnet motors are heat, shock and dirt. The intensity of the magnetic flux of the permanent ceramic magnets is a vital clue to the

Checking a motor by means of an airscrew. "Black box" is an optical tachometer.

28

condition of the motor but it is difficult to measure. As supplied when new the magnetism will be fairly consistent from one motor to another, but overloading the motor with too big a pinion for a couple of heats or consistently throwing the motor from full forward to full reverse will soon build up the temperature until the magnetism is harmed. Shocks from heavy collisions or using hammers to 'tune' things up can also harm the motor. Of course dirt spoils contact between brush and commutator and builds up friction in bearings.

Clean your motor between outings as described above, always gear your buggy on the low side and avoid giving your motor excessive shocks and it should last well. If you wish, it does no harm to take advantage of the magnet 'Re-Zapping' service offered by some motor specialists.

Motor performance checks

There are several pointers to the condition of your motor which can be carried out with great sophistication or with very simple equipment. Condition checkers such as that made by Kyosho are available which usually check two parameters, current consumption with the motor off-load and brush/commutator resistance with the motor running. Such checkers do give a good idea if treatment is needed and can show the results of treatment clearly. My own favoured methods involve more equipment but have the advantage of giving an actual performance comparison from one motor to another. I check motors with an optical tachometer (rev-counter) and good quality 20 amp meter for RPM and current consumption on-load by using model aircraft propellers and very large capacity nicad packs charged between runs using an automatic cut-off charger. First checks can be carried out with the motor off load using a small piece of insulating tape stuck to the shaft to give the optical tachometer something to register on.

Brush pressure can be adjusted with the motor running to give the best compromise between pressure, current consumption and RPM.

Various propellers are then fitted and the RPM and current readings noted; a graph can then be drawn that compares RPM with current which allows quick comparison of one motor's characteristics with that of another and also indicates from one set of checks to the next on the same motor whether the performance has gone off. It is very interesting to do 'before' and 'after' tests when you are preparing motors for a race.

Good quality optical tachometers are not cheap, however, nor is a meter capable of reading up to 20 amps, which is necessary for the checks described. I use a good quality moving coil meter movement with precision shunts attached to allow the meter to measure the largish currents involved. Both moving coil meter and shunts can be obtained from R.S. Components stockists.

Taking it to pieces

The need for regular cleaning has already been stressed and this procedure should be carried out every time a racing session has been completed. It is important that cleaning is done straight away because, if the motor is left, dirty deposits may well become hardened into the internals of the motor. Any moisture present will soon rust the steel parts, in particular ball-races, which will never recover.

If the motor is of the type that can be dismantled, take it to pieces and wash off all parts with a suitable cleaning fluid. I would advise against the use of lighter fuel which I have seen some people using. Although it is a particularly clean form of petrol, it is still *petrol*, with a very low flash point needing only a spark to ignite it, obviously dangerous when buggies are built up and charged up by numerous potential sources of sparks. Very careful use of a worn piece of 400 grade emery paper will remove any traces of discoloration from the commutator, which should be washed scrupulously clean following the use of abrasive.

Once all parts are clean and dry, the motor can be re-assembled and armature bearings lubricated and the commutator treated. If the motor is enclosed in a sealing balloon this should be thoroughly washed and dried before replacing or it may otherwise carry dirt back into the clean motor.

Finally examine the power connections for any signs of deterioration. Regular flexing of the wires where they solder onto the tags of the motor will probably result in one or two strands of the connecting wire breaking. If this happens, replace the wire straight away: each of the tiny strands is important, and for every one that breaks there will be a measurable drop in the performance of the motor, as those remaining are not able to carry the full current efficiently to the motor.

If suppressor capacitors are fitted examine them carefully for cracks. If they are cracked they must be replaced as they are probably no longer doing the job they were fitted for, i.e. suppressing interference from the motor, interference that could prevent your R/C receiver from working properly.

Should your motor be one with a fixed end, i.e. a Standard motor, that you wish to use for competition purposes, then you will obviously

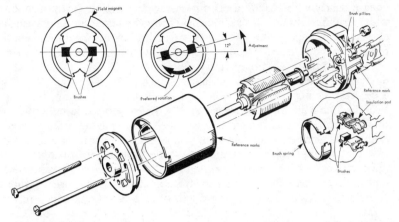

Fig. 10 Some motors are simple to dismantle, as in this illustration, which also shows timing details or "brush lead".

not wish to risk disqualification by dismantling it for cleaning. It is of course possible to both clean and service motors of the open brushgear type without taking them to pieces. Firstly mark the brush holder and brushes so that the brushes can be returned to their correct holders the right way round after the cleaning has been finished. Now remove the brushes and clean the motor in your chosen fluid. Dry off and with a small piece of wood with a scrap of 400 grade emery paper glued to it, polish any traces of discoloration from the commutator. Clean again then refit the brushes and lubricate the motor.

Getting the best from your motor

As far as most buggy racing enthusiasts are concerned actual tuning up or reworking motors is not a practical proposition. The performance of the motor will be determined by the manufacturer or specialist tune-up artist. A motor will be selected on the basis of sales talk, literature or recommendation but all too often the motor that the individual buys does not live up to his expectation. This is very unlikely to be the fault of the motor, as most poor performances are the result of dirt, mistreatment and, most common of all, incorrect gearing.

Providing that the motor is prepared, lubricated and cleaned regularly in accordance with the preceding instructions, it will do what the manufacturer intended, if used properly.

31

Particularly with Modified class motors gearing is of prime importance. Modified motors in addition to having ball-race mounted armatures and a higher quality of balancing usually have variable timing and frequently have thicker gauge armature windings. (Thicker wire= smaller numbers, 22 gauge wire is thicker than 27 etc.) Dealing with thickness of wire first, the electrical resistance of the wire goes down as the wire thickness goes up, which means that more current can flow and theoretically more power can be developed. Although this is usually so, there is a benefit to be gained from having a fairly large number of turns of wire round the poles of the armature, so there is a case for using a double or even triple wound armature. This enables a thinner wire to be used but, doubled up, it packs more compactly into the available space and results in more actual coils of wire winding round the poles and a greater strength of magnetic field, hence more power.

The commutator feeds current to each of the coils in turn, but only for a brief period of time, for each coil could actually consume far more current than is good for it. If the motor is stalled the current flow through the coil will rapidly overheat it, then the insulation burns off, the wire shorts out and the motor is ruined.

For this reason if the motor is restrained or overloaded too much by too high a gear ratio current consumption will go up alarmingly. Heat will build up and the permanent magnets will be spoilt, a vicious spiral of diminishing performance that is to be avoided at all costs.

As for timing, this relates to the position in the rotation of the motor when the individual poles of the armature are actually 'switched on' by the commutator. By switching on the poles early in the cycle it is possible to maximise the strength of the individual poles' magnetic field to give the best possible rotational thrust to the armature. In modified motors this degree of advance is comparatively high but means that if the motor is restrained from revving freely there will be the previously mentioned build up of heat and current consumption.

To make sure that the motor gives of its best always gear on the low side. Use a smaller rather than a larger number of teeth on the motor pinion. Start off with a small pinion and if your buggy seems slow on the straights compared with the others on the track, before fitting a larger pinion first ask yourself if the speed on the straight could be improved by taking the corner on a better line and thus entering the straight at a faster speed. If your buggy will not run for the full length of the race it is possible that the gearing is too high rather than too low. Check the temperature of the motor: if it is too hot to touch the gearing is definitely too high.

Whoops! Two buggies negotiating a fairly rough surface. Picture also gives some idea of the size of track raced on.

Most buggy motors are wound to give a standard 5-minute run on the correct gearing and only if your buggy is running at full racing speeds for a lot over 5 minutes should you consider fitting a larger motor pinion. Only raise the number of teeth on the pinion by one at a time, then try the results. If the acceleration is definitely poor then you have gone too far and should change down a ratio before running the motor into the ground over a full run.

3 Transmission

With a rolling chassis and motor all ready to go attention can be turned to the transmission of the power – reduction gears, differentials, belts, chains and shafts which take the power from the motor to the wheels – looking firstly at the motor and its mounting and the first stage of gearing.

In the chapter devoted to motors the importance of selecting the correct gear ratio was stressed and this usually starts at the motor pinion, as this has the largest single effect over the overall ratio. Gear ratios are expressed in a numerical form, e.g. 3.5:1 meaning, in the case of the motor to primary gearbox, 3.5 turns of the motor will result in 1 turn of the next shaft. The overall gear ratio from motor to wheels is not very often quoted and as a general principle, ratios should not be treated as very important figures. There are too many steps along the way in most buggies to make it at all certain that the ratio or pinion used on Buggy 'A' by driver 'A' will be the same as that used by driver 'B' on Buggy 'B'. For example, if you decide to fit alternative and different tyres to your buggy from those fitted to an otherwise identical buggy driven by the person at the next pit table, don't whatever you do fit the same pinion to your motor as he does if he seems to be going faster than you are. If your wheels are actually larger than his, you will almost certainly overgear your buggy.

Treat your buggy as a unique machine. The gear ratio you need for best results on any particular track on any particular day is a result of the combination of the quality of your nicads, the weight of your buggy, the type of motor you are using, the diameter and even tread pattern of the tyres you choose and your driving style.

34

A selection of pinions and a useful tool, a pinion-puller.

Contrary to some popular opinion, gears are a little more complex than just lumps of metal with pegs stuck around the edges. Even the crudest looking cast metal gears are carefully shaped to a geometrically generated and specific tooth profile. This profile is arrived at by a combination of factors including the diameter of the gear and the number of teeth and it is important for the gears to operate efficiently that gears *designed* for meshing with one another are indeed used. There are two basic types of gears, those made to a Metric Module number and those made to an Imperial (Feet and Inches) Diametrical Pitch (DP) formula and the two will not mix properly. Nor will gears of one module number mix with gears of another module number. This does all sound a little exotic but should serve to convince you that it is important to get the correct gears for your buggy and not just fit whatever comes to hand.

Proper clearance between gears must be maintained and this almost inevitably means that there must be some way of moving the motor back and forth to set the clearance. Some buggies cannot easily be modified to achieve this, so gear manufacturers may have to make specially shaped gears to cope. If motor adjustment is not provided for, the holes in the motor mount can usually be elongated to slots. It will often be necessary to open up the centre locating hole for the end bearing of the motor as well. If slots are made, it will be necessary to put washers under the heads of the fixing screws and they may not be long enough to take the extra thickness. Make sure that any replacement

Elongation of motor mounting holes, including the end bearing location hole, allows adjustment of gear meshing.

screws are the correct thread and that they do not project into the motor so far as to foul the armature or crack the magnets.

Assuming a means of adjustment has been arrived at, how to make the gears run smoothly? Correctly meshed gears will run almost silently so noise is a good indication of poorly meshed gears. There should be just discernible 'backlash' or free play between the gears and careful observation as the motor is moved and the pinions turned should enable you to arrive at a good set-up.

Moving on from the motor pinion to the next stage, ideally all gears should be supported on ball-raced shafts. Most buggy manufacturers make provision for this in the form of accessory packs but, if not, there are ways and means to get round the problems, available from many

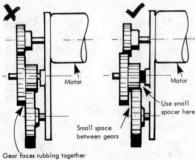

Fig. 11 (left and opposite). Sources of friction in gears and methods of dealing with them.

36

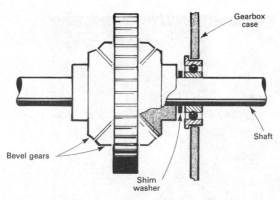

Fig. 12 Use of steel shims on bevel gear shafts.

Gearbox case

Shaft

Bevel gears

Shim washer

specialist suppliers. Differentials are now fitted to or available for most buggies and their use is a must for the serious racer. Bevel gears and bevel gear differentials can as well as helping with the handling of the buggy provide a potential source of friction as there is a tendency for bevel gears to thrust away from one another, putting heavy end loads on the supporting bearings. Ball-races are really essential on either side of a bevel gear diff, particularly if the bearings are used to keep the planetary bevels in correct contact with those on the diff output shafts. Use steel shims to limit the sideways movement of the diff. See Fig. 12. Wherever possible, make sure that the gears are fully protected from dirt. It is not usually necessary to apply oil to plastic gears, but metal gears do benefit from lubrication. There is a 'Dry' spray aerosol made by Rocol that is particularly good for gears in buggies as it tends to prevent dirt becoming stuck to the gears which rapidly causes wear.

Four-wheel drive buggies of necessity have to have some means of transmitting power from the traditional rear mounted motor to the

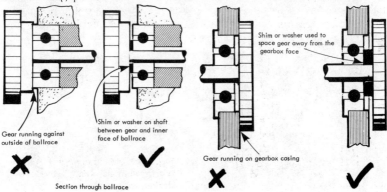

Shim or washer used to space gear away from the gearbox face

Shim or washer on shaft between gear and inner face of ballrace

Gear running against outside of ballrace

Gear running on gearbox casing

Section through ballrace

37

The idler gear on this *Scorpion* is ball-raced.

front wheels. This can be a shaft, toothed belt or chain. From virtually all points of view a shaft is the best method. Even if there is a slight loss of power through the bevel gears usually fitted, the frictional losses caused by the sideways loads caused as the belt or chain expands and pulls the shafts that it connects towards one another will be higher. See Fig. 13. Chains require very little or no tension at all (some guidance is pro-

The "ladder" chain drive is subject to stretching after a comparatively short period of use.

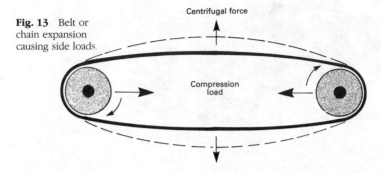

Fig. 13 Belt or chain expansion causing side loads.

Centrifugal force

Compression load

vided in most cases to keep the chain from flying out as it speeds up) but toothed belts really do need some form of tensioner. A loosely fitting toothed belt is likely to slip and will soon be destroyed if this happens. Too much tension is, however, a bad thing, as increased side loads can sap power. Keep a close eye on the condition of the Meccano 'ladder' type chain used for chain drives in most electric buggies. It stretches fairly quickly and once stretched will not fit the teeth of the sprockets properly, making for a jerky and inefficient drive. Simply shortening the chain by a link or two is not good enough as the 'rungs of the ladder' will still not span the sprocket teeth as they should and replacement is the only solution.

Centre drive shafts that carry power the length of the buggy need a small amount of end-float to accommodate movements in the chassis. Set up the drive shaft using a small spring in the drive cup at one end. If necessary you will need to file down the rear of the drive cup to provide the essential end float but it is more than likely that there will be some present. Do make sure that the shaft cannot pop out of engagement. Shim out the drive cup if possible to prevent this happening.

Wheels and tyres

The wheel and tyre together form a vital link in the suspension of the buggy. Wheels should be light but strong enough to do the job without distorting and allowing the tyres to come off. Tyres are a far more variable element, since the material and tread pattern have dramatic effects on the handling of the buggy. Weight of both wheel and tyre are important as they are what is technically known as 'unsprung weight'. Designers always try to keep the weight of all parts of the suspension to a minimum in keeping with strength as the higher the weight the more difficult it will be for the dampers and springs to control the movement

39

The Mugen *Bulldog* is another 4WD buggy from Japan.

and keep the tyre in close contact with the ground. Avoid the temptation to fit heavy metal wheels which look good but are a sure way to spoil the handling.

Buggy tyres need to be fairly flexible if they are to conform to the contours of the ground over which they travel and generally those made out of rubber seem to work best of all, even if they are the most expensive. Tyres must be firmly fixed to their hubs and kept clean. There is no point at all in trying to sort out the handling of a buggy fitted with tyres carrying a caked-on layer of mud, as the grip will certainly be spoilt and the extra weight will do the handling no good at all. The tyres must be fitted to the hub straight and true. Once the tyres are fitted spin the wheel and look to see that they run true. If not, re-fit and check again. Out-of-true tyres cause bad vibration to be set up in the suspension that will destroy the grip as the whole wheel and tyre assembly shimmies across the track surface.

There is a strong temptation to try and fit the tyres from one make of buggy to another, and this is fine as long as a good job can be made of the fitting. Beware of changing wheels from one buggy to another, as out-of-true or loosely fitting wheels will have the same effect as poorly fitted tyres. A poor fit of wheel to axle may also result in damaged wheel hubs. Finally, filling tyres with foam is something to be approached with caution, particularly if racing on a wet day. The foam can soak up a great deal of water, putting up the overall weight of the buggy by a fair amount, never mind destroying the handling. A small hole in the wheel is not a bad idea, as any water that gets into the wheel can be drained out, and leaving the hole open to allow the air to leave the tyre or sealed with a piece of sticky tape adds to the tuning possibilities.

Suspension 4

For the moment it is safest to assume that the designer of your buggy has got things right when it comes to suspension design, so simply concentrate on those parts of the existing system that present opportunities for adjustment and fine tuning. Both Springs and Dampers come under this classification and a lot of benefit to handling can be obtained by spending time getting them right.

Revamping dampers

Let's take a look at the Dampers first. These can be of various types, Constant Volume, One Way, Simple Fixed Volume or even connected up to a reservoir. See Fig. 14. I would recommend that the serious racer invest in a couple of sets of spare dampers so that he can have dampers filled with different grades of oil all ready to slip straight onto the buggy. Well-used dampers may be so worn that the only answer is to throw them away. First check for oil leakages by temporarily filling the damper and operating it for a minute or two in your hands. Any signs of more than a smear of oil on the spindle and you will need to do some restoration work.

Dismantle the damper totally and using well-worn 400 grade water-proof carborundum paper (wet-or-dry) and a drop of oil, polish the spindle thoroughly while it is spun round in the chuck of a power drill. Further polishing with 'Brasso' or similar will really finish off the job. Throw away the 'O' ring seals, which must be replaced with new. If the spindle is scratched, the inside of the 'O' ring will be marked also and

41

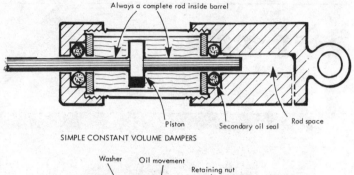

Always a complete rod inside barrel

Piston

Secondary oil seal

Rod space

SIMPLE CONSTANT VOLUME DAMPERS

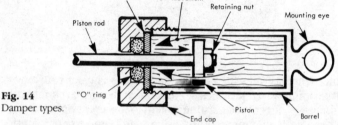

Washer

Oil movement

Retaining nut

Mounting eye

Piston rod

Fig. 14
Damper types.

"O" ring

End cap

Piston

Barrel

will not seal properly. Thoroughly clean all the parts of the damper and reassemble, filling with oil. The range of oils marketed by Robbe are really excellent as they are supplied in convenient dispensers and the grades are clearly marked. It is very helpful to know the SAE or viscosity rating of the oils you are using, for then it is simple to find thicker or thinner grades of oil to experiment with. Anonymous little bottles labelled 'Damper Oil' are not very helpful unless they specify a viscosity.

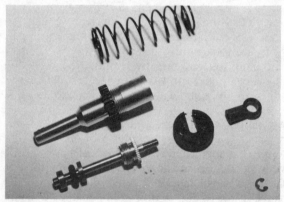

The basic parts of a typical damper.

Polishing the damper spindle.

Bleed all the air from the dampers: you can tell when they are free of air because the damper will operate smoothly from one end of its stroke to the other with a constant resistance. If the damper resistance drops half way through the stroke it is a sure sign that there is still air present. Likewise, if the damper will not reach the extremes of travel then there is too much oil in it and the end will have to be loosened to allow a little to escape.

It is well worth taking the trouble to dust-proof the spindles of your dampers and if coil springs are fitted over the dampers, cover these in as well. Fingers cut from rubber gloves make ideal sleeves and can be held in place with small nylon tie-wraps. Do make sure that the dampers are not fitted in a sloppy manner; if there is a lot of free play in the mountings then bush them with short lengths of plastic sleeving.

Springs

Springs are a lot more difficult to experiment with than dampers, but there are various sources of springs. Try Proops, who sell bags of assorted springs, as does KR Whiston. You will find their addresses in the back of this book. Alternatively take a look at other makes of buggy, since the springs used in other kits may well suit yours and be different in strength.

To start with you must be clear about one or two things. The adjustment made by screwing collars up and down the barrel of a damper adjusts 'Ride Height' or ground clearance, but it does not affect the hardness of the spring. Ideally ride height should be set so that the buggy

43

The Kyosho *Optima* has sharply raked rear dampers.

Fig. 15
(Below). Simple examples of anti-roll bars.

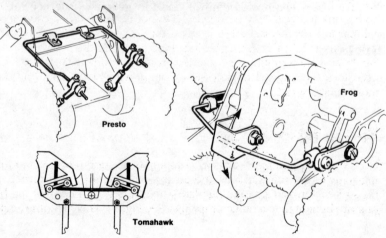

Presto

Tomahawk

Frog

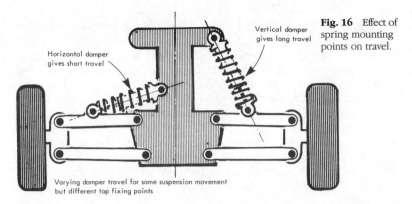

Horizontal damper
gives short travel

Vertical damper
gives long travel

Fig. 16 Effect of spring mounting points on travel.

Varying damper travel for same suspension movement
but different top fixing points

doesn't quite bottom out on the worst humps or dips in the track, and the setting of the ride height will be affected by both the strength of the springs and the grade of oil in the dampers. It is beneficial to keep the buggy as low as possible, that is to say, keep the ground clearance or ride height to a minimum. The higher the buggy is the greater will be its tendency to tip over on corners.

Tipping over on corners is not usually a real problem when racing outdoors, but the buggy can however be seen to roll on corners, indicating that if the roll became excessive, the buggy would indeed turn over. In practice the tyres usually lose grip and the buggy slides before the body roll becomes a turn-over. Body roll in itself is not a problem unless it becomes so great that the suspension can no longer cope. Try driving your buggy round in tight circles close to yourself and see if you can see any signs of any one of the wheels leaving the ground. If you can see this happening then an anti-roll bar either to the front or rear or both front and rear may be needed. Do not be tempted to fit an anti-roll bar just for the sake of it – only use a curative measure if there is a disease present that needs curing! Take a look at the accompanying Fig. 15 and photographs for some ideas on anti-roll bars. You may well need to try a range of thicknesses of piano wire before you find the most suitable grade.

Spring rates

On buggies that employ coil-over-damper suspension units the mounting angle of the unit can have a dramatic effect on the performance of the suspension and a mounting plate with a variety of holes in it can be of more benefit than a range of springs. See Fig. 16. The flatter the angle

45

of the strut the softer will be the action, because for the full travel of the suspension the spring will only be compressed by a very small amount. Progressive rate springs are also worth looking at as they will give nice soft suspension for undulating sections of the track but still provide the high resistance necessary to cushion really excessive bumps and dips. What happens is that the closely spaced coils of the spring are the softer section and these open and close to absorb small bumps but if a big bump is encountered the soft part of the spring firstly takes up the slack then the coils become closed up (coil-bound) and the wider-spaced, stiffer section of the spring starts to come into play. By carefully adjusting the spacing of the coils throughout the length of the spring it is possible to make a spring that becomes progressively harder as it is compressed. See Fig. 17.

Bump Steer

Avoiding minor inadequacies in suspension design is almost impossible and Bump Steer is the result of one such little problem. If it were possible to design a steering set-up that was absolutely symmetrical and fit it into a suspension that was also symmetrical then Bump Steer would not occur. But what happens is that there are small changes in the distance between the servo saver and the steering track rod connection point as the suspension goes up and down. Take a look for yourself and you will see that as the suspension is compressed on your buggy the steering moves, causing the wheels to adopt toe-in or toe-out, depending on the exact way that the steering is hooked up. In

A Tamiya *Fox* lifts its front-wheels as it takes a bump.

Suspension
compression causing
bump steer.

other words, as the buggy goes over a bump, the steering is affected. If
you think about the possible results of this then you will appreciate why
you need to be very careful when making modifications to steering.

Take for example the case of a buggy nose-diving onto the track after
a jump; as the suspension compresses the steering goes to excessive
toe-in and the likely result is to cause the buggy, already unbalanced,
to flip end over end because of the extra drag of the front wheels facing
inwards. Positioning of servo savers is not just a result of convenience,
so do check for the effects on bump steer of any modification you con-
template before finally committing yourself.

Four-wheel steering

With a buggy that has four-wheel or front and rear wheel steering there
is a double possibility of adverse effects arising from bump steer. Kit

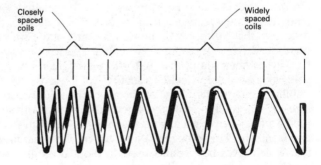

Closely
spaced
coils

Widely
spaced
coils

Fig. 17
Progressive rate
spring.

47

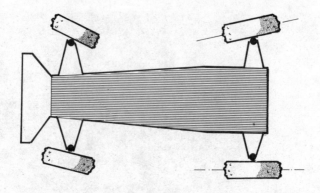

Fig. 18 Distortion of steering for which toe-in and toe-out compensate.

designers will have taken most of the problems on board during initial design and by far the most likely handling problems resulting from rear wheel steering are caused by using too much movement. The amount of movement required to make a big difference in the power-on steering in tight corners is very small.

The tendency for all four-wheel drive buggies is to exhibit understeer in corners, particularly as the power is applied, leading the driver to complain of lack of steering. Add rear wheel steering and this characteristic disappears. Add too much and the buggy becomes unbelievably twitchy and unpredictable down fast straights. The answer is to keep the rear steering to little more than what appears to be toe-in to toe-out proportions as the steering is operated from full lock to full lock.

Toe-in and Toe-out

On the subject of toe-in and toe-out, this is usually set to very small amounts and is little more than pre-set compensation for the amount of distortion that will occur in the various parts of the steering linkage at high speed. See Fig. 18. If front wheels are set to point straight ahead at rest, it has been found that high speed straight running is unpredictable, whereas if the wheels are set to point inwards slightly (toe-in) the stability is much better. Drag of the track surface and castor action of the steering will tend to force the wheels towards toe-out so a little more toe-in than appears actually necessary is set in. With four-wheel drive and front wheel drive buggies either toe-in or toe-out may be tried and that which gives best results used. Toe-out does give an extra bit of

48

Rear suspension and anti-roll bar of the Marui buggy.

steering on the inside wheel of a corner and toe-in extra steering on the outside wheel so the effects of toe-in and toe-out should be monitored during cornering as well as while speeding down the straight.

Making the changes

If you are quite certain that you are going to be able to really tell if suspension changes are having any effect and have understood the part that all the components of the suspension play in keeping your buggy on the track you should make all of the changes that you decide upon in a logical and controlled manner. The ideal suspension system will allow the chassis of the buggy to travel in a smooth path while the wheels move up and down to accommodate the unevenness of the track. For the suspension to do its job properly it needs to be fixed to a strong and stiff chassis, otherwise the chassis itself will twist and bend, masking the function of the suspension.

Any modifications to the chassis must be made with this in mind. By all means try to achieve a lighter chassis but do not remove material that is required for stiffness. Box section chassis tend to be the stiffest and also often provide the most scope for lightening, as large flat areas of material without any cut-outs add little to strength but a lot to weight. It may in fact be better actually to increase the weight of the buggy by adding stiffening ribs so that the suspension works better.

The dampers are very important, as they absorb the forces generated as the wheels are forced up and down by bumps and dissipate the energy in the form of heat. The oil in the dampers becomes warmed up as the damper pistons move up and down and it is beneficial to use quite thin grades of oil, as the viscosity changes from cold thick oil to hot, and thin oil will not have such a noticeable effect on the handling as a race progresses. The function of the springs is to keep returning the suspension to its central position after displacement and they should be just strong enough to overcome the resistance of the dampers. By pressing the car down to the suspension stops or dropping it from a few centimetres above your work surface you should be able to gain an initial impression of the balance between springs and dampers. The buggy should rise to its normal ride height without any tendency to bounce after dropping. If the rise is slow then the damping is too effective, and conversely, bouncing up and down before settling indicates an under-damped situation. If the chassis is not returned to its correct ride

A lightened chassis on an Associated RC10.

height at all then the springs are probably too soft. A 150-200mm drop should test the suspension to its full compression and back again. The springs and dampers should be capable of extending the suspension fully once the weight is taken off the buggy and for this to occur not only will the dampers need to be filled with the correct grade of oil and the springs be of the right strength, the pivots will have to be in good order too.

Try out suspension modifications on a well-known track in conditions that allow you to assess results properly. Don't make modifications on a wet day when you normally drive in the dry and beware of trying to completely alter a proven set-up on a track that you are not familiar with, unless you are very experienced at making alterations and know precisely what you are looking for.

Make only one change at a time and check out the results very carefully by driving enough laps to convince yourself that the changes have had an effect. It may be that because the effect is to make the buggy initially more difficult to drive an instant reaction would be that the modification was a bad one. Do try for long enough to really check this out. It may be that your buggy was altogether too soggy in its responses

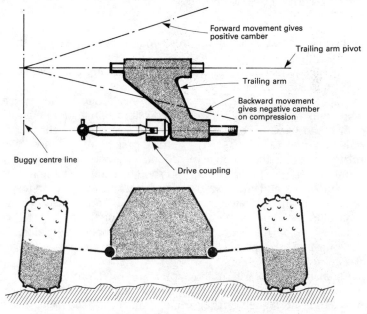

Fig. 19 Effect of pivot pin angles on wheel camber.

The Hirobo *Tomcat* uses a belt-drive system.

in the first place and you have actually made an improvement that just needs getting used to.

The buggy has got to be responsive but not unpredictable. A soggy steering response makes it easy to drive but won't allow you to make the rapid and precise corrections that will sneak you past the opposition while they struggle to drive an unpredictable animal of a buggy.

In broad terms, once you have got the suspension right there will only be minor variations from one track to another and those will be related more to the amount of ground clearance and steering lock required. On very bumpy tracks you should change to a thinner grade of damper oil and increase the ride height, possibly changing to a progressively harder rate spring, both changes aimed at absorbing the forces generated by the bumps without allowing the chassis to bottom out. Very smooth tracks need altogether less suspension travel and hard damping and hard springs coupled with very low ground clearance will pay off.

On many buggies with trailing arm suspension, pivots for both front and rear suspension arms are angled. Varying the angles of the pivots will affect the wheel camber quite dramatically. See Fig. 19. It is beneficial to arrange for negative camber to be present when the sus-

Half a dozen buggies entering a corner. A pile-up seems inevitable among the back four – not a good place to be.

pension is compressed, mainly to aid grip during cornering. It is not detrimental to performance to have a slight amount of toe-in or toe-out on rear wheels so do not be put off from making experiments with rear suspension that will cause these. You will find the results interesting and often well worth the trouble of drilling alternative mounting holes etc.

Although most buggies with four-wheel drive have equal ratios for both front and rear wheels there may be a benefit in trying higher ratio rear drive particularly if there are free-wheel clutches fitted to the front wheels. In this situation the buggy becomes mainly two-wheel drive but if the rear wheels slip then the roller clutches engage and front-wheel drive comes into action. This can help in cornering and many 1/8 scale circuit racing cars have this feature. Of course to make this type of modification is not all that easy: different sprockets or toothed belt pulleys will be needed and a small lathe is a definite advantage when it comes to making this type of change. I have found the Unimat 1 to be very useful in this respect and it costs less to buy than most buggy kits. You will find addresses for suppliers of gears, sprockets and timing belt pulleys at the rear of the book.

5 Power supply

Nickel Cadmium (nicad) fast charge cells are the heart of the electric-powered buggy. Six cells are assembled to form a battery, the equivalent of the fuel tank in engine-powered vehicles. It stands to reason that with only a partially full (partially charged) battery, the buggy will not run for as long as it would were the 'tank' to be full. The rechargeable battery is an electro-chemical device that works by changing the chemicals to one particular state in the battery by charging and then by connecting a load (the motor) across the battery, changing the chemical state back again as the battery discharges.

The detailed construction of the internals of the cell dictates its characteristics, and by and large the greater the area of active positive and negative electrode that can be crammed into the cell case and the more

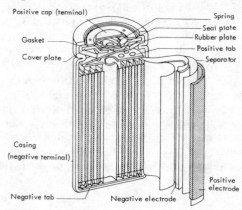

Positive cap (terminal)
Gasket
Cover plate
Spring
Seal plate
Rubber plate
Positive tab
Separator
Casing
(negative terminal)
Negative tab
Negative electrode
Positive electrode

Fig. 20 Nicad cell construction. Reproduced courtesy Sanyo Marubeni (U.K.) Ltd.

54

substantial the internal connections from electrodes to cell terminals, the faster the cell can be charged and discharged and the greater will be its capacity for electrical storage. See Fig. 20.

As nicad cells are most definitely a mass-production item, each particular size rolling from the individual manufacturers' plants in many thousands if not millions, then there will be a great deal of uniformity from one cell to another with very well documented performance characteristics. Manufacturers of these cells do understand their products very well indeed and although we might like to think that as buggy racers we have a better idea of their performance in our particular situation than they have, making such assumptions and then going against their advice, on charging methods in particular, is foolish.

What cells to buy?

Although there is great uniformity in performance from one cell to another, there is also no doubt that mass-production techniques do result in a spread of quality and performance and realising this, the manufacturers are able to grade their products initially using known characteristics to predict likely variations in performance. This usually results in some cells being sold under one serial or type number with others sold as something else. Therefore it is virtually certain that every cell you buy will be in some sense 'selected' during its manufacturing process.

It is well worth pointing out at this stage that most experienced and successful buggy-racing competitors will say that sets of cells rarely begin to indicate their true quality or give of their best until they have had a 'breaking-in' period of up to 20 charge/discharge cycles and any selection process that is made at the point of manufacture must be subject to some degree of unreliability.

By and large, if you buy cells from a well-respected manufacturer such as Sanyo, Saft, Ever-Ready or General Electric, you will have a quality product that has the potential to power your buggy to success. Some types of cells do most definitely have characteristics particularly well suited to certain types of racing: those cells of known high current release characteristics will benefit on tracks that are very tight and twisty, the cells that are recognised as being very good on duration will benefit on fast flowing circuits.

As well as the charge and discharge characteristics of cells you will be faced with a choice between cells already made up into packs in several different configurations or supplied singly. There are equally as many

Various forms of battery pack, courtesy MacGregor Industries.

valid arguments for both approaches, ready-assembled packs or single cells. My own preference is for single cells but I must say that if you are not sure of your ability to make very rapid and totally reliable solder joints using a very large soldering iron, then go for ready assembled packs every time. If you do choose to assemble the packs yourself you will be able to fit heavier connecting links between the cells than those fitted by the manufacturer, which are often barely adequate for the currents that buggy owners expect to draw from their cells.

I use lengths of solid copper wire to connect cell to cell, and 16swg can carry the current required with ease. You will need to clean the contact areas on the ends of the cells thoroughly with emery cloth and ideally use a flux that is recommended for use with stainless steel. An acid flux such as Baker's Fluid will do, however, but must be totally cleaned off after the job is finished. Keep the interconnecting wires to a

Heavy-duty metal strap cell-connectors spot-welded in place.

minimum length and tin the ends and the joint areas on the cells before actually making the joint. When all is ready, very quickly solder the joint. Only a couple of seconds are needed if you use an iron of at least 70 watts. Any longer contact with the cells will cause a local heating which may cause permanent damage. Once the joint has been made, clean off the flux with methylated spirits. The cells can then be sleeved, using heat-shrink tubing, into sticks and the sticks held together with silicone rubber, super glue or glue from a hot melt glue gun before sleeving is added over both sticks and the end electrical connections are made.

Don't be fooled into believing that problems of poor duration, indifferent acceleration and slow speed are necessarily the result of bad cells. The first suspect must always be you, the driver and tuner of the buggy. No matter what cells you use, if you drive badly or fit the wrong gear ratio, your buggy will be an indifferent performer.

Exactly the same should be said about charging techniques. I have yet to come across a set of cells that will not run one of my own buggies for 5 minutes when properly charged. There is no magic charging technique that will compensate for a badly prepared buggy and you would do well to spend the time, money and effort required to perfect a super-special charging system in preparing the buggy properly in the first instance and only worry about the latest charging developments when your machine is totally reliable and you make no mistakes in driving a 5-minute race!

That being said, there are ways of charging batteries that are to be recommended and those that are not; if you are indeed serious about competition then you must of course be able to charge your batteries

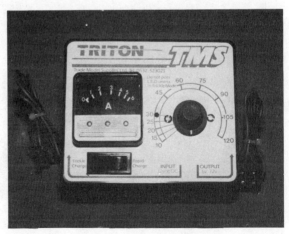

With a clockwork timer and choice of trickle or rapid charge the TMS *Triton* covers most situations.

properly. Although there are many pet methods of charging batteries around and many types of charger, a system that detects the peak voltage under charging conditions is to my mind the simplest, most reliable and cost effective for general use. There are automatic chargers that operate on the Peak Detection principle but it is quite possible to charge to a peak voltage without such a device with some advantages. This method relies on monitoring the voltage at the actual nicad while the charger is connected up to it, using a very sensitive volt meter. As the cells approach their fully-charged state the voltage reading, which has been rising slowly throughout the charge, will start to rise much more rapidly, indicating that a peak voltage is approaching. Ideally the charge should be stopped just before the peak is reached, but this is obviously difficult, certainly for the first time that it is done, for there will not really be any indication as to how high the voltage is going to rise!

The method of supplying the charging current is not critically important. A simple resistor charger with a timer can be easily used and because the technique demands the user's presence during its end stages (to switch off!) the timer has the advantage of allowing the user to go away, come back and either monitor the peak voltage before the charger switches off, or if the charger has already switched off, start up again and then monitor voltages. Alternatively, a simple resistor or resistors can be used but will need constant monitoring. Using a pair of resistors of 0,5 and 1 ohm value, the highly regarded 'Step Charging' technique can be simply carried out.

This method is simply to charge the cells at around 6 amps for 8

A range of C.S. pulse and automatic chargers.

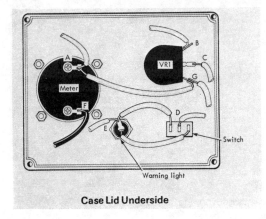

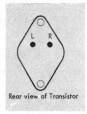

Rear view of Transistor

Case Lid Underside

Warning light

Switch

Meter

Fig. 21 Constant current charger (see also overleaf).

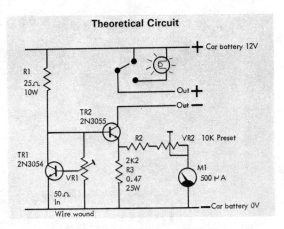

Theoretical Circuit

Car battery 12V

R1 25Ω 10W

Out +

Out −

TR2 2N3055

R2 2K2

VR2 10K Preset

TR1 2N3054

VR1

R3 0.47 25W

M1 500 μA

50Ω In

Wire wound

Car battery 0V

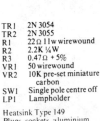

TR1	2N 3054
TR2	2N 3055
R1	22 Ω 11w wirewound
R2	2.2K ¼W
R3	0.47 Ω + 5%
VR1	50 wirewound
VR2	10K pre-set miniature carbon
SW1	Single pole centre off
LP1	Lampholder

Heatsink Type 149
Plugs, sockets, aluminium
cast case for VR1
Insulating kits for
transistors

minutes, then drop the charging rate to 3 amps for 8 minutes, then 1 amp for the final period during which time the peak voltage should be monitored. Resistors of ½ and 1 ohm used singly and together will drop the charging current as required.

I must confess that such methods do not suit me, I still use a combination of Constant Current charging and Automatic Cut-Off charging, I have a home-built Constant Current charger (see Fig. 21 for circuit and component list) plus a Cord Auto Charger and use the Constant Current to charge the battery for the first 15 minutes at 4 amps, then change to the Auto Charger to finish off. With a clockwork timer in circuit I can

Fig. 21 continued.
Constant-current charger
placements.

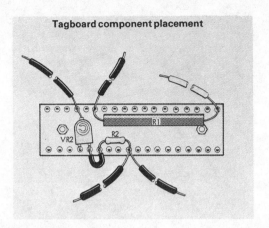

Tagboard component placement

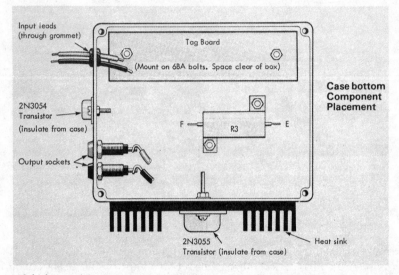

Input leads
(through grommet)

Tag Board

(Mount on 6BA bolts. Space clear of box)

**Case bottom
Component
Placement**

2N3054
Transistor
(insulate from case)

F   R3   E

Output sockets

2N3055
Transistor (insulate from case)

Heat sink

safely leave the constant current charge and the remaining charge can be done in the last few minutes before the race. This system has the benefit of allowing me to set a cooling off period before the race. The last few minutes of charge will not be at a high rate and the battery will be fairly cool before I actually use it.

Temperature of batteries is something that must be checked continually. Remember that the actual active bits of the battery are buried inside heat-shrink sleeving, maybe a plastic box, metal cases etc., and any sign of heat on the outside of that lot indicates a very much higher temperature inside the cells. If the cells become overheated, either through overcharging or over-discharging, which can happen if the cells become short-circuited, then the chemicals inside the cell can 'boil', generating gas which escapes from the cell and cannot be replaced, causing lasting damage.

Sanyo now make a cell that includes a sensor inside that has an external connection to allow a special cut-off charger to be triggered when the cell gets too hot.

A very major point that has to be remembered when using peak voltage detection methods of charging is that the *actual voltage is not relevant, it is the peak that is important*. The actual peak voltage, whether it be 9,5 or 10,5 volts, is irrelevant to the condition of charge; it is more an indication of the state of the battery supplying the charge current and the condition of the nicads. Generally high peak voltages do however show that the nicads are past their best. Do not allow your better judgement to be warped by listening to figures for peak voltages obtained by fellow-competitors while they are charging their nicads, as they might well be using fresher 12 volt accumulators or lower resistance chargers than you are.

Maintaining your nicads

When a pack of nicads is first purchased it will to all intents and purposes be totally flat. What you do with it next will probably set the pattern for its future performance. Immediate fast charging is generally felt to be a bad thing and a 12-16 hour charge should be given at the C/10 rate (where C is the Capacity of the battery, 1200 mAH, giving a charge of 120 mA). Any less a rate of charge will not fully charge the battery however long it is kept on charge.

Once slow charged like this run your buggy with a low gear ratio so that the battery is not overloaded and do not discharge to the absolute end point where your buggy comes to a dead halt. Allow the pack to cool down completely before recharging and do not charge at the fastest rate available to you: a 1 or 2 amp charge, stopping well before the peak voltage is reached, will be adequate. Three or four runs to initially break in the battery can be followed by steady build-up to a full charge and a steady improvement in performance of the pack should be noticed.

It is likely that the first outing will only result in three or four runs and the pack will then have a rest until the next outing. My own prefer-

61

ence is to leave the pack alone at this stage, partially charged, until the night before the next outing, when I trickle charge at the 120 mA rate overnight. Once the pack is fully broken-in there are various courses available. I am suspicious of the technique that calls for the cells to be discharged and then left with a load resistor across them as, if this is done with the cells as a complete pack then there is a possibility that at least one cell in the pack will become reverse charged.

What happens is that the better cells in the pack hold more charge than the others and when the worst cells are actually totally discharged there is still some life in the better ones. These better cells will continue to discharge through the poor cells and, remembering that the cells are connected in series (positive to negative, see Fig. 22), the poor cells may become reverse charged until the whole pack reaches a stable level which apparently is 0 volts if a volt meter is put across the pack. In fact, several cells could be at a 'Plus' level and the remainder at a 'Minus'. Those at a minus level could be permanently damaged during storage. However, if the cells are discharged to an equal voltage individually then the idea of storing with a load resistor across the pack is possibly valid. To discharge the cells individually is simple enough if small windows are cut in the sleeving between the cells so that probes can be inserted and connection made to a load of some sort, either a light bulb or a small motor – anything in fact that discharges the battery. Monitor the voltage whilst this is going on and when it reaches 1 volt do the next cell until the whole pack is fully and evenly discharged. Before next use, trickle charge at 120 mA and you will have a well-balanced pack that should easily give you the power to compete successfully.

Do keep the connectors on your pack spotlessly clean. A small layer of oxide could lose you up to ½ volt from the pack. In an ideal world gold-plated connectors would be used, but tinplate is more common! A spray with a contact lubricant is a good idea while the connector is still new, and replacement when it becomes a dark grey colour or the tin wears off and rust starts to show is a must. Examine the wiring where it enters the connector and if there is any sign of broken conductors the necessary repairs should be made, likewise for damaged insulation.

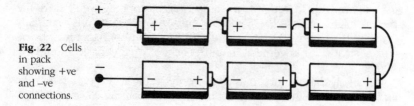

Fig. 22 Cells in pack showing +ve and –ve connections.

Checking out battery packs

I use the same technique and the same test rig for checking out battery packs as for motors, except that the observations I make are different. A motor that is past its peak is best used, since, after all, there is no point in using up the life of a good motor just to flatten battery packs, is there? The procedure is simple enough but requires a little preparation and organisation if it is to be reliable. Proceed as follows:

(a)   Set up your chosen motor with a smallish propellor on it, 6in diameter and 3in pitch is about right.

(b)   Prepare a piece of paper with columns for time, RPM and voltage.

(c)   Charge up your pack to full capacity using your normal charging procedure.

(d)   Connect up to the motor and start a clock and the motor simultaneously.

(e)   Note the pack voltage, the motor RPM and the current reading in amps every 30 seconds, taking the readings in the same order each time.

As soon as the voltage drops below 6 volts on load stop the motor and note the time of switch-off. You will now be able to plot a graph of the discharge performance of the battery pack under test and, using the same technique, prepare similar graphs for each of your packs. Figure 23 shows graphs of several battery packs. There are now much more sophisticated ways of carrying out this same procedure using micro-computers, but essentially the job done is as described above, the main difference being that the computer is programmed to do the graph

A mains-input
charger with timer,
by Weston U.K.

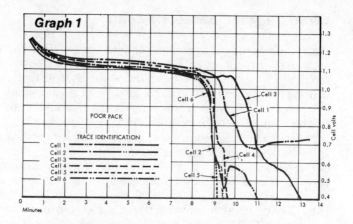

Graph 1
Pack voltages

Pack Voltages Mins.	Voltages
0.5	7.709
1.0	7.495
2.0	7.330
3.0	7.278
4.0	7.218
5.0	7.147
6.0	7.059
7.0	6.952
8.0	6.820
9.0	6.610
10.0	5.559
11.0	4.260

Graph 2
Pack voltages

Pack Mins.	Voltages Voltages
0.5	7.173
1.0	6.977
2.0	6.839
3.0	6.791
4.0	6.752
5.0	6.704
6.0	6.646
7.0	6.568
8.0	6.417
9.0	4.186
10.0	2.273
11.0	1.634

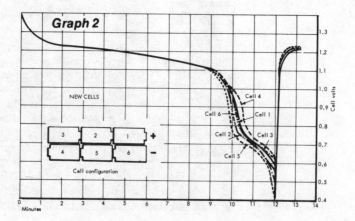

Fig.
23

64

drawing and print out a report on the cell's performance at the end of the test.

To really make the tests even more meaningful, they should be carried out on individual cells, then a set of fully matched cells could be assembled from all those tested.

Pulse charging

For some years it has been accepted that charging cells by giving them bursts of heavy charge followed by periods of rest can result in better cell performance. This process is known as pulse charging and there are several commercially available chargers on the market. They tend to be expensive compared with the simple resistor and timer methods, but have given good results.

Nicad 'memory'

Memory is a well-documented and understood characteristic of nicad cells. Put simply it means that if the cells are continually only discharged to, say, half, then eventually they will only be capable of giving half their rated capacity. They will have developed a memory which tells them that they need only give out so much before packing up! It is possible to break this memory effect if it does develop but in most buggy applications it is not very likely. The usual method of restoring the pack to its full capacity is to break the memory cycle by several cycles at full charge to full discharge.

The memory effect will be apparent on the first cycle but will gradually diminish until the cells have almost fully recovered. It is felt that once the cells have developed a memory they will never really be top performers again. The best remembrances to give the cells are obviously those of full and happy charge and discharge cycles with no overcharging and no reverse polarity-inducing over-discharges.

Nicad safety

Nicad cells are capable of producing extremely high currents on discharge, and short-circuits within packs or just in the wiring of your buggy can be disastrous. Although many commercial buggies did at one time fit fuses, their use in competition buggies is virtually unheard of,

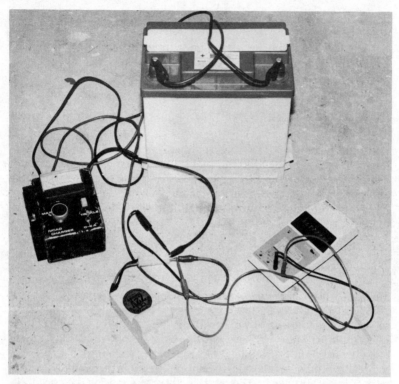

Charging from a 12v car battery is normal and often necessary at outdoor tracks. Here a constant current charger (left) is hooked up to the battery pack (foreground) and a digital voltmeter (right) is added to the circuit.

for the simple reason that the current flow for very short periods when full power or full reverse are given, particularly with modified motors, is likely to blow any suitable fuse. The same current applied for a longer period of time would probably start to seriously overheat wiring and damage speed controllers but for a short period, the buggy can take it.

As there is no fuse, any direct short of the nicad pack will cause high currents to flow in the wiring, high enough for the usual size of connecting wire to glow red hot, certainly hot enough to melt insulation, probably hot enough to cause fire if there are combustible materials touching the hot wiring.

If a short does occur, the evidence will appear very quickly – a small amount of smoke, a smell from melting insulation, maybe even a noise of 'frying'. Don't wait and watch, ACT! Cut, rip or wrench out the connections between the sticks of the cells if they are in reach, or if not and the short is within the pack break the pack open with anything to hand, a big screwdriver, anything. Now break the connections between the cells somewhere within the pack. It is more important to destroy the short-circuit than preserve the nicads, which are probably ruined within a few seconds of the short occurring anyway.

Remember, the wiring will be very hot, and so will the cells be. Beware of touching any part of the electrical wiring of the car with bare hands if there is a short within the buggy.

As well as there being a danger from heat, the short may also cause dangerous build-up of pressure within the cells. The excessively fast discharge can cause the cells to produce gas which builds up inside the cell and although the cells are vented, the vent or safety valve may not relieve the pressure before the cell case fails explosively. The same pressure build-up can also arise as a result of overcharging. The first sign of heating should be monitored carefully and if heat continues to build up even after the cell is taken off charge, then it should be cooled quickly by plunging into cold water – preferably in the open air as once started the heat build-up can cause short-circuits to occur inside the cell which will eventually result in the cell either venting or, in extreme cases, exploding.

While in no way wishing to be alarmist, I feel it only right to stress the dangers involved in abusing nicads. There have been very few instances of the occurrences described, but where explosions have occurred, they have usually been as a result of abuse and not correct use.

6   Radio

There comes a time when many buggy drivers feel that the original 'budget' priced R/C equipment they started out with has become due for replacement. There are so many gadgets and gimmicks built into the top of the line equipment these days that it is difficult to believe that they are not useful!

Having decided that an update is due, then the decision has to be made as to whether to replace everything, or just the transmitter. There is no reason why this should not be done, and most manufacturers supply individual components for their R/C systems. You should of course realise that you cannot mix Amplitude Modulation (AM) and Frequency Modulation (FM) systems. You must use an FM receiver with an FM transmitter and vice versa. Nor will the two systems mix when it comes to operation, incidentally, as they will interfere with one another; you cannot operate AM and FM on the same frequency at the same time.

While it is generally completely practical to operate a transmitter from one manufacturer with a receiver from another there may be minor problems of incompatibility caused by non-matching crystals. It is essential that the crystal pairs supplied by the *receiver* manufacturer are used in both transmitter and receiver.

Of course, you may decide to retain your existing servos and use an alternative transmitter/receiver combo, or retain everything but the servos. Both these courses of action will certainly require a change of plugs on switch harness and servos. It is important to be totally sure that you understand the colour coding of the servo and battery leads before attempting this particular job. Colour codes for the major manufacturers are shown in Fig. 24. The three wires for the servo are two power

A basic two-stick transmitter with, in front, receiver, two servos and receiver battery box.

supply lines (positive and negative) and the signal wire, the wire that carries the decoded information from the receiver to the servo amplifier. The +ve and −ve wires are connected through the receiver straight to the battery, so any mistake in connecting up will put full battery volts the wrong way into your servo . . .

Fig. 24 Servo lead colour codes

Manufacturer	Positive	Negative	Signal
Futaba	Red	Black	White
J.R.	Red	Brown	Orange

Sanwa
  (Flat ribbons)
	Grey Tracer	Centre
		  conductor
			Outside
			  conductor

Acoms	Red	Black	White

To fit a new plug, strip wire, twist ends and tin. Slide on heat-shrink tubes. Solder leads, then slide tubes over joints and shrink. Complete by sliding additional tube over whole joint and shrink (not shown).

Fitting servo plugs

Before starting you will need a small soldering iron, about 15 watts, a pair of Bib or similar wire strippers, heat-shrink tubing, cored solder suitable for electronic work, a pair of small pliers and a rubber band.

A fully-equipped two-stick set of radio gear.

Cut off the plug from the servo and strip the insulation from the wires for about 3mm. Twist together each core on all three leads and tin the conductors with solder. Prepare the ends of the wires from your new plug in the same way.

Now cut off 4 short lengths of heat-shrink tube and slide one over all three of the wires. Push this well away from the actual joint area. Now slip a rubber band over the handles of your pliers to keep the jaws closed. Slide a length of heat-shrink over the +ve wire of the servo lead and grip this in your self-closing plier, which will leave you with two hands free, one to manipulate the soldering iron, the other to hold the +ve wire on the new plug lead and position the tinned end against that of the servo lead. Heat up the joint area with your iron and the two tinned leads will fuse together. Repeat this operation for the remaining two wires, check that they are correctly matched up then slide the three heat-shrink sleeves down over the joints and either apply heat from your soldering iron or use a hair drier to shrink the tube. Last of all, slide the fourth piece of tube down and shrink this over the whole set of wires to give added protection and support to the joints.

Designed expressly for car racing, pistol-grip transmitters have been introduced by two or three manufacturers.

Reversing servos

Although there are reversing switches fitted to more and more transmitters, you may decide that you still wish to keep a favourite transmitter that does not feature this facility. There are occasions that arise when in spite of all your best efforts the only way to achieve a satisfactory hook-up of servo to steering or speed controller is to fit a servo that rotates in the reverse direction to both those that you have spare. Do not despair, it is possible to reverse the direction of rotation of the servos. It is not easy and it does demand skill with a soldering iron, and a pretty small soldering iron at that. Do not attempt to carry out the reversing operation with anything bigger than a 15 watt iron and in very bright light conditions. The printed circuit boards in the servo are very small and the components very closely packed together; a mistake can ruin the servo amplifier. Proceed as follows:

(1) Remove the servo case bottom. Be careful not to disturb the gearbox while doing this otherwise you will make your task doubly difficult as you will suddenly find you need to reassemble a servo gearbox as well as do a wiring job!

(2) Locate the motor and the power wires from the amplifier PC board. There will usually be two but there may be three. Identify the two that go to the motor brushes, which will be the two that are 180° apart.

(3) Reverse the polarity of these two wires. Use your soldering iron quickly and neatly. It should not be necessary to add any additional solder to the terminals.

(4) As well as the wires to the motor there will be three more wires (apart from the servo connecting lead wires, that is) which connect the amplifier to the feedback potentiometer or 'pot' as it is usually called. Find these and trace them to the feedback pot. Note that the wires are connected to three terminals that are arranged approximately as shown in Fig. 25. Draw a neat pencil sketch of the exact arrangement in your servo, labelling the wire colours and making sure there is a reference

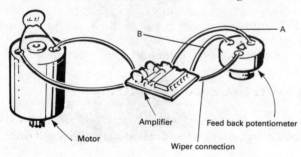

Motor
Amplifier
Feed back potentiometer
Wiper connection

Fig. 25 Servo internal wiring between motor, amplifier and pot.

for the correct way up of the servo in relation to your sketch. Those labelled A & B must be reversed, they are the wires that go to each end of the track of the pot.

Once the two sets of wires are reversed, the servo will run in reverse. Check your job for neatness and accuracy before returning all the parts to the case and checking out. It is a good idea to make sure that the servo is not hooked up to your buggy before switching on, as it will probably want to adopt a new centre position, and any restraint may stall the motor and do damage. Be prepared to switch off instantly if there is any sign that the servo has stalled or if there is no sign of life at all!

If the servo does not work, first check that it is not jammed up by trying to turn the output shaft gently. If it is jammed against the stops turn it to an approximately central position and switch on again. If the servo runs to one end of its travel and jams you have almost certainly made a mistake in changing over the feedback pot wiring. Refer to your sketch and make sure that you did actually reverse the correct pair of wires. In reversing many dozens of servos I have yet to find one in which I could not identify the correct wires to change over and I have yet to have a failure. It can't be all that difficult – I'm no electronics expert.

Centring servos

Servos with separate or splined output shafts are unlikely to need any adjustment for centring after reversing but those with square output shafts almost certainly will. There may be a centring adjustment down the centre of the output shaft, which will be in the form of a screwdriver slot and can usually be seen by looking down the fixing screw hole in the output shaft. If this is the case a slim screwdriver is inserted down the hole and with the servo plugged in and the system switched on the screw is turned to bring the output shaft into line.

Other types of servo may have an additional tiny skeleton pre-set pot in the amplifier to adjust the centre or it may be necessary actually to adjust the feedback pot. This is done by loosening the fixing screws and twisting the body of the pot until the output shaft comes into alignment.

Doing away with the receiver battery

If you have decided to fit an electronic speed controller it will be fitted with a regulated power supply for the receiver. The controller will need

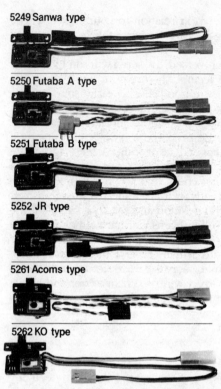

5249 Sanwa type

5250 Futaba A type

5251 Futaba B type

5252 JR type

5261 Acoms type

5262 KO type

A range of regulators to suit various types of equipment is manufactured by Tamiya.

to be fitted with a plug to fit your receiver and this should be done in accordance with the instructions above. The controller instructions will tell you which wires are to be connected to the receiver and what function each colour wire is to perform. There is only a single three-wire connection from the controller to the receiver, two of these being the +ve and −ve power running from the controller to the receiver and supplying power for both receiver and steering servo. The third wire, the signal wire, carries the signal back to the controller.

Alternatively you might either fit a self-contained voltage regulator or a much simpler diode. The regulator has the advantage that it will continue to supply current for the receiver when the drive batteries are almost totally flat, while the diode will stop working when the drive batteries are still capable of driving the car leading to the occasional out-of-control car.

A single diode is often used, but this can provide rather a high voltage to the receiver and for safety's sake it is preferable to use two,

The Parma resistor speed controller. A diode can be seen top left. See also Fig. 26.

connected end to end. Diodes are marked with a band to indicate direction of current flow and this should be on the side nearest the receiver. If you do get the diodes the wrong way round no damage will result, they just won't work! Diodes are usually fitted in conjunction with a resistor controller and are sometimes supplied as standard fittings on buggies. Resistor controllers are still very popular for buggy racing as they are cheap in comparison with electronic controllers and easy to repair and trouble-shoot.

Although fitted to many kits as standard equipment, the types of resistor used do not always stand up to the demands of racing and in particular of modified motors. Ceramic cored resistors of the Parma type are by far the best sort to use and can be bought as a complete pack of parts to build up into a controller. Different values of resistor are available, ½, ¾ or 1 ohm usually. The lower value will give a very quick response to throttle opening but the higher values are most suitable for slippery tracks, the ¾ ohm being a good compromise.

The resistor can be fitted to a bracket taped to the servo or can be fitted to the car in place of the type supplied with the kit. A heavy duty wiper arm and contact button will be needed and it is a good idea to fit a second wiper arm to trap and hold the moving wiper onto the full power band of the resistor so that really good contact is made at full speed. I always tie the wire onto the moving wiper with a small tie-wrap to avoid constant strain on the solder joint. A full wiring diagram is shown in Fig. 26 for fitting a resistor control with micro-switch reverse.

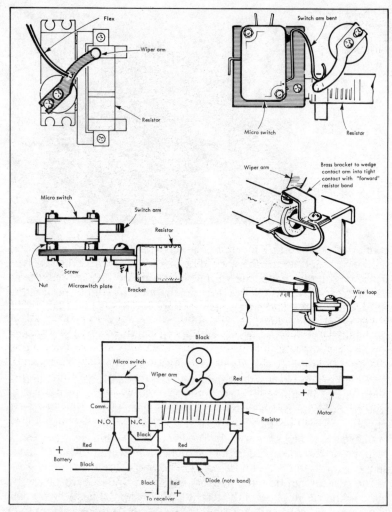

Fig. 26 Microswitch reverse and resistor control.

Electronic speed controllers

Properly installed and used without abuse, electronic speed controllers are by far the most elegant solution to speed control of a buggy. The 'black box' just plugs into the receiver, there are no exposed parts to get

The C.S. speed controller from Germany.

dirty and need servicing, adjustment is simple and of course the controller will incorporate a receiver power supply. The disadvantage is expense, particularly with some of the latest Field Effect Transistor (FET) units now popular. The FET is a particularly efficient high current transistor which is used as little more than a solid-state micro-switch switching large currents at very high speeds to give a very fast response. All electronic controllers hate abuse, particularly incorrect wiring up. Reverse polarity at the input will destroy the electronics almost instantaneously, but if diodes were to be fitted to protect the unit then the voltage drop resulting would destroy the high efficiency. The answer is care. Read instructions meticulously several times with the unit in your hand, checking that you understand exactly which wire is

A British "black box", the Fleet FPS14 controller.

Heat-dissipating case contains MacGregor controller.

which before making any attempt to connect up. It is not a bad idea to label each wire as you identify it with a piece of masking tape with its function written on it. I recommend properly shielded plugs for the connections; using spade connectors and the like is all very well for the expert but even then I have seen 'experts' connect up the wires the wrong way round in the panic moments before the start of a race. Keep all wiring to a minimum length, for even the best connecting wire has a resistance and excessive length will drop the voltage available at the motor as well as adding unnecessary weight to the buggy.

Try to adopt a logical system of wiring up, and use sockets for output and pins for inputs. On battery packs and speed controller outputs there will be sockets; on motor, speed controller input and charger/discharger there will be pins. By this means you will be able to connect motors directly to battery packs for testing and quickly change motors without having to change plugs or resort to soldering.

Radio frequencies (in Britain)

At the time of writing the frequencies available for use with buggies are the 27MHz band and the 459MHz Ultra High Frequency bands, although it is probable that soon after this book is published there will be 40MHz frequency allocations from the Government. It is illegal to use any other frequencies. Even though there is no requirement to obtain a licence to use model radio control equipment, this does not mean that there are no laws governing its use, there are! Use of any frequency other than those allocated by the authorities renders the user liable to prosecution with very heavy fines possible plus the confiscation of equipment.

The Laser controller
gives some idea of
complexity.

It is irresponsible in the extreme to use illegal frequencies. There are legal users of almost all radio frequencies who do not take any more kindly to their use by buggy drivers than buggy drivers take to those who use their own legally-allocated frequencies. By reversing crystals, illegally importing special crystals or using non-legal frequency band equipment you are breaking the law and contravening the rules of the National Association (BRCA) which governs the buggy-racing sport. Remember also that you may well be keeping bad company if you decide to go illegal, since if you happened to turn up at a race meeting with another illegal frequency user there will be no sympathy from the race organisers if you suffer mutual interference and no time given for you to try and sort matters out.

When you do decide to enter the big world of open competition you must make sure that you have alternative frequency crystals before you get to the race. Organisers have a difficult task sorting out frequencies for racing heats when there may be up to 100 drivers and cannot always accommodate the driver who cannot change frequency. At least one alternative should be available and the well equipped racer will build up a complete set of crystals.

On the track

Having a well prepared buggy and a fully understood charging system is only half the picture when it comes to race winning. There are many things that have to be considered and mastered before success is likely to come your way. I don't for one moment suggest that race winning can be learnt from a book, but there are a number of points of advice that can be and should be heeded before going racing.

It is as well to be prepared for something of a surprise when you go to a major race meeting for the first time. Most drivers will appear to be lapping at speeds far in excess of anything that you are able to achieve. Don't be put off, there are probably many reasons why and it is up to you to use your skill to catch up and pass them.

Not the best place –
dusty, and if the front
buggy stops...

101 excuses for not having gone faster

The most important lesson to be learnt about racing is not to kid yourself. It is all too easy to blame a poor performance on indifferent nicads, a poor motor, wrong gear ratio or even bad marshalling – anything but the true reasons. Remember that you bought, cared for and charged the nicads, you maintain the motor, you selected the gear ratio and made the stupid mistake that caused your buggy to become stuck on a track marker. Watch the experts. How many times do they ever get stuck and need marshalling? Your success is almost entirely in your hands and it is no use blaming others for your failures.

10 ways of going faster

Enough of that sort of talk, the whole point of this book is to help you achieve success. If you have absorbed the rest of the book you should by now have a buggy in perfect fettle ready to race with the best of them and win.

One of the great secrets of fast driving is smoothness. The truly quick driver rarely looks as though he is trying very hard: there are no violent slides or near-disastrous collisions with other cars or obstructions, just smooth rapid progress. This smoothness can only be achieved by thinking about the car, the track and the other competitors continuously, by driving to a plan which is still able to be modified as the race progresses.

A positive attitude towards the race helps and is largely a result of thorough preparation and a confidence in your own ability. Nothing is more unsettling than the nagging thought in the back of your mind that goes along the lines of 'I wonder whether that dodgy connector on the nicad pack will come undone?'

Nerves affect almost everyone who climbs onto the drivers' rostrum. You are on show, about to reveal the full extent of your skill in public and the knowledge that others will criticise is always there in the back of your mind. There are no pet answers to the nerves problem. It is said that the release of adrenalin into the bloodstream that gives the 'butterflies' feeling is intended to speed up reactions and therefore without that feeling being present we are unlikely to give of our best anyway.

That's all very well, but if you can barely hold your transmitter for shaking then the whole thing gets to be a bit too much. My own answer is to have a strict routine before the start of each race to occupy my

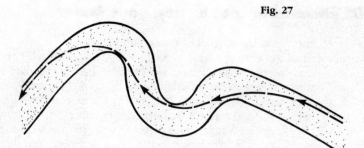

Fig. 27

mind and not allow the adrenalin to get the upper hand. I fully check the wiring, wheel nuts, motor pinion grub-screw and lubricate those points that need it. I fit the body shell, being careful to put in the clips so that head-on collisions will push them further in rather than out and generally visually check the whole buggy. That done, I put all my tools in their proper places, tidy up my table and then it's time to race. Any panic immediately before a race is sure to make things worse, since a calm, concentrated frame of mind is essential to a good performance. One final comment, in my own case nerves have become less of a problem with advancing years and greater experience.

In no particular order, here are some 'Golden Rules':

(1) Slow 'in', fast 'out'. This refers to cornering technique, where it is vital to choose a line round each corner that allows the buggy to smooth out the bend to as near a straight line as possible. See Fig. 27. Even so, enter the corner too fast and it becomes very difficult to keep to the best line. The buggy then is sure to exit the corner on a bad line and probably sideways as well, meaning that it first has to be straightened up before power is applied, spoiling speed down the following straight.

(2) Choose a good line. Lines through individual corners are important but each single corner is just a part of a whole series of corners. Make a mistake leaving one bend and the next becomes difficult to negotiate. If your line is spoilt, slow down sufficiently to get back into the correct groove before making your next bid for the lead.

(3) Five mistakes can cost you a lap. Take the average 5-minute race, maybe 20 laps? Take the average crash – maybe 3 seconds for the marshall to reach your buggy, put it on the track and for it to regain full racing speed. How many mistakes can you afford to make? Better in fact to let the hot-shot driver in front gain 2 or 3 metres on each corner and then crash than try to keep up with him and crash yourself.

(4) Watch the lights. If there are starting lights as well as a horn watch

Don't concentrate so hard on your corner line that you don't notice a converging rival!

the lights and not your car for the vital start to a race. Remember that light travels faster than sound and you will have a split-second advantage by watching, not listening, that can put you into the lead. As long as you know precisely where your buggy is in the start line-up it should not be difficult to spot when you flick your eyes back – after all, it will be the leader, won't it?

(5) Let others make the mistakes. Don't ever be impatient when it comes to overtaking. If you are driving quicker than the buggy in front all you usually need to do is stay really close behind for a few corners to get him rattled enough to make a mistake, then you slip by. The last thing to do is to use force to pass or try to out-drag the opposition down the straight and into the corners. The usual outcome is a spin off into the track markers. The best place to overtake is almost always on the exit to a bend once you have pushed your opponent so hard that he has overstretched himself going round the bend and has been forced to slide wide to the outside, losing both line and balance.

(6) Smooth power. It is often the case that the inexperienced driver will drive quicker with a standard motor than with a modified motor. Quite simply the tendency to bang the throttle wide open with a

modified motor should be curbed unless the buggy is pointing in exactly the right direction. Otherwise, the result will be a buggy that is sliding wildly from side to side across the track with wheels spinning as the slower, standard motor equipped buggy accelerates smoothly away down the straight. In general, power should be applied progressively unless the buggy is really well balanced.

(7) Only start the race once. Each start from a standstill uses enormous amounts of the limited stored electricity in your nicads, eventually spoiling speed on the straights and even allowing buggies that started the race more slowly than yours to pass and win.

(8) Plan your driving. Avoid power-wasting stoppages, if you see a pile-up in front of you slow right down – if you didn't see it, you are not driving well at all, you must keep a wary eye on the track at least one bend ahead of your buggy. If you hit a buggy stationary on the track you are to blame in most cases, you ought to be able to watch the track far enough ahead to stop at whatever speed your buggy is travelling at.

(9) Only drive as fast as you need to. Really this only applies to Finals when the aim is to be first across the line. In heats where a fast qualification time is needed you will obviously need to drive at top speed throughout the race. By all means build up a lead but once a good lead has been established then relax a little, let the others make the mistakes in their desperate attempts to catch up. You may well find that even after relaxing the effort a little you still pull away as your driving will almost certainly be smoother and more considered.

(10) Know your limits. It should take no more than a couple of corners behind or in front of a faster buggy for you to realise that you can't compete. Don't try to win this time, there will be another occasion when your buggy will be the faster, when you will have that 'everything's just right' feeling and your turn will come to be the winner. Allow faster buggies to go past and never try to race the race leader as he laps you. You might take him off the track and remember, that's where you're going to be at the next race meeting!

Appendix 1
British and American suppliers

Company	Type of Business	Products Handled	Catalogue
Ripmax Models Ltd. Ripmax Corner Green Street Enfield Middx.	Importer, Distributor	Kyosho Kits, Futaba R/C	Yes *
Irvine Engines Ltd. Unit 2 Brunswick Industrial Park Brunswick Way New Southgate London N11 1JL	Importer, Distributor	Sanwa R/C, AYK & Mugen kits	*
Model Flight Accessories The Mill Mill Lane Worth Deal Kent CT14 0PA	Manufacturer, Distributor	Saft nicads, MFA Chargers, MFA Electro Throttle	*
A1 Batteries Co. PO Box 103 Stockport Cheshire SK4 3EW	Distributor & Retailer	Saft nicads	Yes
MacGregor Industries Ltd. Canal Estate Langley Slough Berks. SL3 6EQ	Manufacturer, Distributor	JR R/C equipment, Saft nicads, MacGregor electronic speed controller	
G. K. Models 390 Holdenhurst Road Bournemouth BH8 8BL	Retailer	All goods related to 1/10 buggies plus own brand accessories etc.	Yes
SRM Racing 140 West Street Fareham Hants.	Retailer	Associated RC/10 specialist plus many specialist imported accessories	

Appendix 1 (continued)

Company	Type of Business	Products Handled	Catalogue
Dave Nieman Models 34 Watford Road Sudbury Wembley Middx.	Distributor, Retailer	Hirobo Kits	
Harden Associates Millet Street Bury Lancs.	Distributor	Challenger R/C	
Harry Brooks 13/15 Victoria Road Portslade Sussex BN4 1XP	Importer, Distributor	Sprengbrook & Multiplex R/C	
Whistons New Mills Stockport Cheshire	Mail order supplier	Surplus and new materials, metal, wire, nuts, bolts, springs etc.	
Proops Brothers Ltd. 52 Tottenham Court Road London W1P 0BA	Retailer	Surplus nuts, bolts, tools, springs, electrical parts	
Daval Gear Co. Ltd. Welham Green Hatfield Herts. AL9 7JB	Manufacturer, Retailer	Gears, chain drive sprockets, timing belts and pulleys	
Nodis Racing Developments 28 Brunwins Close Wickford Essex	Manufacturer, Retailer	Gears and differentials	
Ashbourne Technology 8 Conyers Way Great Barton Bury St. Edmunds Suffolk IP31 2RL	Manufacturer, Retailer	Speed controllers, chargers	
Helgar Racing 18 Manor Farm Drive Chingford London E4 6HJ	Manufacturer, Distributor	Parma products	Yes
RIKO Ltd. Old High Street Hemel Hempstead Herts.	Importer, Distributor	Tamiya 1/10 buggy kits, Acoms R/C and accessories	

Company	Type of Business	Products Handled	Catalogue
Windsor Model Shop 45 Albany Road Windsor Berks.	Retailer	Specialist buggy shop	
Nics Kits 3 North Street Martock Somerset TA12 6DH	Retailer	Specialist buggy shop	
Supercharge Models 29 Church Street Romsey Hants SO5 8BT	Retailer	Specialist buggy shop. Computer program for Commodore 64 timing	
MG Model Products 91 Clearmount Road Weymouth Dorset DT4 9LF	Manufacturer, Distributor	MG motors	
Star Electronics 1-3 Garfield Terrace Broughton Road Stoney Stanton Leics. LE9 6JA	Manufacturer, Distributor	Speed controllers, chargers	
Fleet Control Systems 47 Fleet Road Fleet Hants. GU13 8PJ	Manufacturer	Fleet R/C and speed controllers	
Morley Models 10/12 Morley Bottoms Morley W. Yorks. LS27 9DQ	Retailer, Manufacturer, Distributor	1/10 buggy specialist, charger and accessory manufacturer	Yes
Intronics Beechdale Challow Close Hassocks Sussex	Manufacturer, Retailer, Distributor	Intronics speed controller and chargers	
Phil Greeno Models Ltd 9 Village Way East Rayners Lane Harrow Middx.	Importer, Distributor, Retailer	S.G. of Italy. Specialist R/C Car shop	

Appendix 1 (continued)

Company	Type of Business	Products Handled	Catalogue
Amerang Ltd. Commerce Way Lancing West Sussex BN15 8TE	Importer, Distributor	Marui 1/10 kits	
Mardave R/C Racing 7 Heanor Street Leicester	Manufacturer	Mardave Kits for 1/8 & 1/10 buggies	
Demon Products 79 Northumberland Road North Harrow Middx.	Manufacturer, Distributor, Retailer	Demon speed controllers, Demon motors, Sanyo nicads	
Laser Products 230 New Road Booker High Wycombe Bucks.	Manufacturer	Laser speed controllers, pulse chargers	
Cecil Schumacher Rudge Church Brampton Northants. NN6 8AU	Manufacturer, Distributor	Buggy kits, CS chargers, GRP sheet material	Yes
Ted Longshaw Model Cars 7 Warren Road Chelsfield Orpington Kent	Importer, Distributor, Retailer	Everything to do with R/C cars	Yes
PB Racing Products Downley Road Havant Hants. PO9 2NJ	Manufacturer, Distributors	Manufacturer of 1/8 & 1/10 scale buggies	
Howes 9-10 Broad Street Oxford OX1 3AJ	Retailer	1/10 buggy specialist	
Moulding Research Company Oldington Trading Estate Stourport Road Kidderminster DY11 7QP	Manufacturer	1/8 & 1/10 tyres	
Tru-Tyres 31 Broadhurst Gardens Eastcote Ruislip Middx. HA4 9QJ	Retailer	Motor overhaul service	

Company	Type of Business	Products Handled	Catalogue
Specialist Turned Parts Unit No. 3 National Trading Estate Bramhall Moor Lane Hazel Grove Stockport SK7 5AA	Manufacturer, Retailer	Specialist parts for Tamiya and Associated	

Major U.S. Buggy Manufacturers

Cox Hobbies, Inc.
1525 E Warner Ave.
Santa Ana, CA 92705

CRP (Custom Racing Products)
2500 Woodbridge Ave. PO Box 267
Edison, NJ 08817

RPS/Yokomo
1655 E Mission Blvd.
Pomona, CA 91766

Parma International
13927 Progress Parkway
North Royalton, OH 44133

Model Racing Products
12700 Northeast 124th St. 17
Kirkland, WA 98033

Playtron, Inc.
PO Box 3242
Sandimas, CA 91773-7242

Raco Modelcraft
1421 E Saint Andrews Place
Santa Ana, CA 92705

Monogram Models
8601 Waukegan Rd.
Morton Grove, IL 60053

Great Plains/Kyosho
PO Box 4021
Champaign, IL 61820

Bo Link RC Cars
420 Hosea Rd.
Lawrenceville, GA 30245

AYK Racing USA
PO Box 3479
Mission Viejo, CA 92690

Associated Electrics
1928 E Edinger
Santa Ana, CA 92705

Delta Mfg.
27 Race Car Court
Lorimar, IA 50149

Tri Star Imports, Inc.
PO Box 11392
Santa Rosa, CA 95401

Appendix 2
Motors, controllers and chargers

Table 1 Motors

Manufacturer	Type	Label	Turns	Gauge	Ballraces	Timing	£ Price **
Mabuchi	RS540	MG Buggy Special	25	0,7mm	No	Fixed	11.95
	RS540SD	Tamiya Black	*	*	*	Fixed	17.99
	RS540SD	Tamiya Enduro	*	*	*	Fixed	17.99
	RX540SD	Tamiya Technipower	*	*	2	Adjustable	29.95
	RX540SD	Tamiya Technituned	*	*	2	Adjustable	29.95
	RS540	Various	27	28g	No	Fixed	6.95
	RS540S	Various	*	*	*	Fixed	8.95
Kyosho	240S	Le Mans	19	0,90mm	2	Adjustable	19.95
	480S	Le Mans	24	0,80mm	2	Adjustable	19.95
	480T	Le Mans	26	0,75mm	2	Adjustable	19.95
	360PT	Le Mans	19	0,90mm	2	Adjustable	29.95
	600E	Le Mans	30	0,70mm	No	Adjustable	12.95
Yokomo		Demon Buggy Single HT	27	*	No	Fixed	11.95
		Demon Mr T	Double	*	No	Fixed	11.95
		Reedy Standard	*	*	2	Adjustable	39.95
		Reedy Sprint	*	*	2	Adjustable	39.95
	Orange Dot	Demon Modified	Double	*	2	Adjustable	38.00
	Silver Dot	Demon Modified	Double/23		2	Adjustable	38.00
	Gold Dot	Demon Modified	Double/19		2	Adjustable	38.00
	Green Dot	Demon Modified	Quadruple Wind		2	Adjustable	38.00
		Demon Special	Double/22		2	Adjustable	*
		MG Buggy Special†	27	0,75mm	No	Fixed	11.00
		MG Red Dot†	Double/24	0,53mm	No	Fixed Ad.	11.95
		Parma Porsche			No	Fixed	11.95

		Parma Renault	(35/23 or 28/22 winds available on Parma motors)				
		Porsche Turbo					39.95
		Renault Turbo					39.95
		Parma Green Label					39.95

AYK							
MG Buggy Clubman	25	0.7mm	2	Adjustable	18.00
MG Magnum (Built to customer spec. winds range from 35 23awg to 18 turn triples, all tested)				Adjustable	39.95
Master Blaster	25	22	2	Adjustable	34.95
GK Models 367	22	0.8mm	2	Adjustable	39.95

Notes
* No information available from manufacturer at time of writing.
† Race-ready, run-in and checked.
** Prices correct at time of going to press but may vary; they are included for comparative purposes.

Table 2 Speed controllers

Manufacturer	Type No.	Name	Facilities	Power Rating	Weight	Size, mm	Price** £
Demon	2BH	*	(Prop. Fwd & Fixed Rev)	*	80g	72×50×20	39.95
	2DH	*	Fixed Rev	*	80g	74×35×27	39.95
	FET	King[7]	(Fixed Rev with relay)	*	70g	65×35×27	*
Laser		Compact	3, 4, 5[8]	*	90	Shrink wrapped	39.95
		Comfet Bug	2, 4, 5	*	65g	Shrink wrapped	49.99
		Comfet Fwd Bug	1, 4	*	40g	Shrink wrapped	59.99

Table 2 (continued)

Futaba	FPMC106B	2, 4, 6	*	82g	2 parts – 15×52×26 & 21×50×37	59.95
	FPMC6B	2, 4, 6	*	82g	2 parts – 15×52×26 & 21×50×37	65.00
	FPMC6	2, 4, 6	*	82g	2 parts – 15×52×26 & 21×50×37	55.00
MFA	Electro	2, 4, 5	*	*	57×50×31	18.50
Parma	Heavy Duty Resistor – servo operated flat wire wound resistor					
Fleet	Speed Control	2, 4, 5	20 amps	*	66×38×36	
	Universal	2, 4, 5	12 amps	*	66×38×36	
MacGregor	MR15M	2, 4, 5	15 amps	*		
Intronics	Firefly GT	2, 4	*	*	57×48×30	42.50
	Firefly MOSFET	2, 4, 5	*	*	*	48.50
Star	Quasar	2, 4_9	25 amps	60g	60×37×29	37.95
	Pulsar	3, 4_{10}	25 amps	80g	66×42×28	29.99

Notes

Speed controllers fitted with forward power control FET transistors do not need Turbo relays as this is the transistor equivalent of the relay but is faster, will not wear out and lose efficiency, also consumes less power.

*No information available at time of writing.   **See footnote to Table 1.

1. Forward only
2. Forward/Reverse
3. Forward/Reverse with Turbo relay
4. Receiver power supply
5. Proportional brakes with reverse at full stick travel
6. Time delay reverse operation
7. 8 power FET transistors fitted
8. Reverse can be selected at any time but does not engage until motor has stopped going forwards
9. 2/3 of full power in reverse
10. Dead stick braking

92

Table 3 Chargers

Manufacturer	Type or Name	Input Voltage	Output Current	Trickle Charge	Principle	Meter	D.'cb'rge Facility	Timer	Price** £
Acoms	AP33	12	Approx 3a	No	Resistor	No	No	Yes	22.50
Kyosho	Multi Charger	12	3 amp cont 6 amp int	Yes	Variable current	Yes	No	Yes	35.00
TMS	Triton	12	3	2 hr max	Resistor	Yes	No	Yes	15.95
	Powertron	240	5	Yes		No	No	No	25.95
Jester	Hercules	12	See Note 1	Yes	Peak Volt Detect.	Yes	No	Auto	24.95
	Goliath	12	4	Yes	Resistor	Yes	No	Yes	15.95
Laser	Pulse	12	6	Yes	Pulsed Output	–	–	–	25.95
MFA	Monitor	12	*	Limited time	Resistor	Yes	No	Yes	16.95
	Transformer – to adapt the Monitor Charger to 240 volt mains operation								15.95
	Mains Rapid	240	5	Yes	–	Yes	No	Yes	32.95
CS	DVM	12	4 Constant	No	Peak Volt Detect.	Yes	Yes	No	69.00
	Standard	12	4	No	Peak Volt Detect.	No	Yes	No	44.00

Table 3 (continued)

Intronics	Clubman	12[2]	4	Constant	Yes	Automatic	No	No	No	19.95
	Peak Detect 12		4	Constant	No	Peak Volt Detect.	Yes	No	No	*
Schumacher	PC1	12[3]	5		Yes	Peak Volt Detect	No	No	No	33.00
Star	Auto Pulse	12		Constant	Yes	Pulsed output	No	No	No	19.95
	Super	12	5		Yes	Peak Volt Detect.	No	No	No	19.95
JME	Auto	12[6]	4		No	Auto	No	No	No	16.95
	Auto Pulse	12[6]	4		No	Pulsed output	No	No	No	19.95

Notes

(1) Hercules is used in conjunction with a range of resistors to give outputs from 0,7 to 5,7 amps.

(2) Can be usd with a 4 amp mains voltage battery charger to provide the input.

(3) Full input and output polarity protection.

** See footnote to Table 1.

Index